WINNING AT COLLECTIVE BARGAINING

Strategies Everyone Can Live With

William L. Sharp

A SCARECROWEDUCATION BOOK

The Scarecrow Press, Inc.
Lanham, Maryland, and Oxford
2003

A SCARECROWEDUCATION BOOK

Published in the United States of America
by Scarecrow Press, Inc.
A Member of the Rowman & Littlefield Publishing Group
4501 Forbes Boulevard, Suite 200, Lanham, Maryland 20706
www.scarecroweducation.com

PO Box 317
Oxford
OX2 9RU, UK

British Library Cataloguing in Publication Information Available

Library of Congress Cataloging-in-Publication Data
Sharp, William L.
  Winning at collective bargaining : strategies everyone can live with /
William L. Sharp.
    p. cm.
  "A ScarecrowEducation book."
  Includes bibliographical references (p.) and index.
  ISBN 0-8108-4733-7 (pbk. : alk. paper)
  1. Collective bargaining—Education—United States. 2. Collective bargaining—
Teachers—United States. 3. School personnel management—United States. I.
Title.
LB2844.57.U6S55 2003
331.89'0413711'00973—dc21

                                                                2002156161

⊗™ The paper used in this publication meets the minimum requirements of
American National Standard for Information Sciences—Permanence of Paper
for Printed Library Materials, ANSI/NISO Z39.48-1992.
Manufactured in the United States of America.

To my father, William B. Sharp, an educator and administrator for forty-three years, who fortunately retired before the collective bargaining law was passed and put into effect.

CONTENTS

PREFACE

This book is about collective bargaining and strategies that can be used successfully in the process. It is written for two groups: (1) practitioners who actively negotiate or those who may be involved in negotiations in the future and (2) graduate students enrolled in courses in collective bargaining or personnel in educational administration.

Those who are practitioners—board of education members, superintendents, negotiators, school attorneys, and other school administrators—may be interested primarily in chapters 4 through 10, which deal with roles in negotiations, the process and strategy of negotiations, procedures for negotiations, nonverbal communication, win–win negotiations, school strikes, and contract management. These chapters discuss practical and specific suggestions for successful negotiations.

Professors teaching graduate courses involving collective bargaining will probably want to add chapters 1 through 3 and chapter 11 to those chapters mentioned previously. Chapter 1 discusses the history of collective bargaining in both the private and public sectors, and looks at the similarities and differences between those sectors. Chapter 2 gives one example of a state collective bargaining law and defines several of the concepts involved in collective bargaining law. Chapter 3 discusses unfair labor practices and describes the typical state laws and procedures regarding these practices. Chapter 11, the last chapter in the book, is unique in that it is a simulation suitable for a typical classroom situation. It includes a description of a school district and community, some relevant facts about the present teacher contract, a list of items to be negotiated, and instructions for the professor. This is a good culminating activity for a course in collective bargaining.

This book is a revision of a volume published by a different publisher and under a different title. The book has been updated with descriptions of recent unfair labor practices, the addition of new references, the inclusion of recent research on collective bargaining, and a new chapter on nonverbal communication.

My background is in school administration: I served as a superintendent of schools in Indiana and Illinois, an associate professor of educational administration at the University of Akron, and a professor of educational administration at Southern Illinois University at Carbondale and am currently professor of educational leadership at Ball State University in Muncie, Indiana. Thus, the book has been written from the viewpoint of management negotiating for a board of education. While this is an admitted bias on my part, it should be recognized that most of the graduate students using this book will be in an educational administration course, and that most of the practitioners using the book will be administrators or board members. So, the bias seems appropriate.

With the exception of chapter 7 and the two essays in chapter 8, the views expressed in this book are mine.

ACKNOWLEDGMENTS

I would like to acknowledge those reviewers who contributed to the development of the first edition of this book (published under a different title and by a different publisher): David R. Friedman, University of Wisconsin, Madison; Thomas E. Glass, Northern Illinois University; William C. Heeney, Stephen F. Austin State University; John R. Hoffman, Southern University, Shreveport; James A. Livingston, California State University, Sacramento; Ivan D. Wagner, Ball State University; and Phillip Young, Ohio State University. Also, Paul L. Tavenner, senior editor at Brown and Benchmark, the publisher of the first edition, was very helpful throughout the entire project.

I would also like to thank Cindy Tursman of ScarecrowEducation for her encouragement and helpful suggestions for this edition.

HISTORICAL PERSPECTIVE ON
COLLECTIVE BARGAINING

This chapter gives a historical perspective on both private- and public-sector bargaining, including the beginning of formal negotiations between teachers and boards of education. It also begins the discussion of state collective bargaining laws, a discussion continued in the next chapter.

NINETEENTH CENTURY–1960S: THE PRIVATE SECTOR ERA

The history of collective bargaining in the public schools begins with the early attempts to organize labor in the private sector. Only when bargaining was well established there did public institutions begin to see the beginning of collective bargaining.

It is believed that American unionism can be traced back to the workers in the crafts and skilled trades, which originated with the European guilds. The first such guild to be developed here was probably the shoemakers' guild, around 1648, in Boston.[1] These early unions were illegal and were often prosecuted for criminal conspiracy, until the Massachusetts court decision in *Commonwealth v. Hunt* in 1842.[2] The postal workers formed the first federal employee organization in 1863 in New York. As a national organization, this group encouraged Congress to pass the Lloyd–LaFollette Act in 1912 to guarantee federal workers the right to organize and petition Congress regarding grievances.[3]

In 1857, school superintendents established the National Teachers Association (NTA) as a professional, almost antiunion organization. These superintendents encouraged their teachers to join the organization; some school districts even required new teachers to join the NTA. Later, this organization joined with other teacher groups to become the National Education Association (NEA). Because some teachers felt that they had grievances that would not be heard by this administrator-run organization, they pulled away from the NEA and formed the American Federation of Teachers (AFT) in 1916. Some of the old school rules seem very outdated today, but some examples may help explain why teachers established the AFT: some state laws prohibited teachers from smoking, some told them what to wear, other imposed curfews on teachers, and at least one even specified how many hours of sleep a teacher should have each night.[4]

In the first part of this century, many people believed that employees, especially those in the public sector, should not have the right to organize, to negotiate collectively, or to go on strike against their employers (as with the 1880 walkout of teachers in Pennsylvania).[5]

Calvin Coolidge, as governor of Massachusetts during the Boston police strike of 1919, stated that there was "no right to strike against the public safety by anybody, anywhere, any time." In 1937, Franklin Roosevelt described a strike by civil servants as "unthinkable and intolerable."[6]

In 1947, Ohio passed the Ferguson Act, prohibiting striking against public authority. Those who chose to go on strike anyway were subject to severe penalties:

1. the striking employee was fired;
2. if rehired, the employee could not be paid more than the compensation had been before the strike; and
3. if rehired, the employee was on probation for two years.[7]

In the same year, the Ohio Supreme Court ruled that a city could not agree to deduct dues from union members. (This law was not changed by the legislature until 1959.)

In 1912, as mentioned before, Congress took a significant first step when it approved the right of the postal workers to form unions. (It should be remembered that these postal workers were federal employees, while public school teachers have always been considered state employees, due to the interpretation of the Tenth Amendment to the U.S. Constitution that education is not a federal interest but should be reserved to the state governments. As a result, each state has in its state constitution a statement recognizing its responsibility for education.)

A second national law, the Railway Labor Act, was passed in 1926 and required those railway employers to bargain collectively with the unions, which were also allowed under this act.[8]

While both of these early laws were significant, they were also very specific: they applied only to two groups of employees. In 1935, a law was passed that had even greater applicability. The Wagner Labor Act (National Labor Relations Act) gave private employees in industry the right to bargain legally. It also instituted the National Labor Relations Board (NLRB).

The NLRB, among other things, could establish procedures for determining what group was the duly elected, exclusive representative of the employees. The board also outlawed "unfair labor practices" (ULPs) by employers against employees and employee unions. (The legal basis for establishing the NLRB as having jurisdiction over collective bargaining comes from the commerce clause of the U.S. Constitution.) Fifty years later, many state legislatures established a similar board to deal with public school bargaining.

Between 1935 and 1947, collective bargaining increased in the private sector, since employees were guaranteed the rights to join unions and to bargain. In 1947, the Taft–Hartley Act was passed, an act that gave employees the additional right to refrain from joining a union. This law was more management oriented than previous laws and placed some restrictions on employee organizations as well as on employers. Under this act, employers were prohibited from:

1. discriminating against employees who chose to participate in a labor organization;
2. pressuring employees who organized or bargained collectively in choosing their representatives;
3. refusing to bargain collectively with the union elected by the employees; and

4. taking action against an employee who testified in a case before the NLRB.[9]

But, as stated previously, restrictions were also placed on the employee organization (union). Among other things, employee organizations were prohibited from:

1. pressuring the employer to discriminate against an employee or to fire an employee;
2. influencing an employer's selection of its representatives for collective bargaining with the union;
3. refusing to bargain in good faith; and
4. pressuring nonunion employees to join the union. (They have the right to refrain from joining a union or joining in union activities.)

Just as the Wagner Act established ULPs against employers, the Taft–Hartley Act included ULPs against unions.

The current significance of these restrictions is that today's state school bargaining laws (where present) contain much of this language, almost word for word from the 1947 Taft–Hartley Act[10]

In 1959, Congress passed an amendment to the Taft–Hartley Act called the Landrum–Griffin Act. Along with the 1947 act, this act expanded the jurisdiction of the NLRB by setting minimum standards of democratic procedures for unions, establishing responsibility for the conduct of internal union activities, and holding union officers responsible for the safety of union funds.[11]

A 1967 court decision, *McLaughlin v. Tilendis,* considered a case in which one teacher had been dismissed and another's contract had not been renewed because they had belonged to the AFT. This decision held that the school board's action violated the teachers' right to free association and due process under the First and Fourteenth Amendments.[12]

1960S–PRESENT: THE PUBLIC-SECTOR ERA

While all the previously mentioned changes in labor relations/collective bargaining were initiated by Congress or the courts, three important executive orders were issued by presidents. In 1962, President John Kennedy issued Executive Order 10988. This order affirmed the right of federal workers to organize and negotiate, but it also affirmed that they did not have the right to strike. (An interesting concept contained in this order is that the employees needed a 60 percent majority of eligible voters to elect an exclusive representative, while private industry needed only a simple majority.)[13] This order included in its scope teachers who worked for agencies both in the United States and in schools overseas. Since public school teachers were state employees (not federal), this order did not legally affect them. However, led by the NEA and the AFT, teachers began lobbying state legislatures to pass state laws giving them the right to organize, to negotiate, and eventually, to strike.

The second executive order (11941) was issued by President Richard Nixon in 1970. This order established the use of binding arbitration to solve impasse situations for federal employees.[14]

While both of these executive orders were criticized by some people because they lacked provisions giving the right to strike, they did give public school teachers ammunition to influence state legislators on the issues of organizing, bargaining, and binding arbitration at the state public school level.

In 1993, President Bill Clinton issued an executive order (12871) expanding the mandatory scope of bargaining to include greater numbers, types, and grades of employees at the federal level and even to extend to the "technology, methods, and means of their conducting their work."[15] This executive order also recognized that the traditional adversarial relationship between labor and management was outdated.[16]

As with many "firsts," there is sometimes a debate about which school had the first collective bargaining agreement, which had the first union, and which was the first to go on strike. Part of this debate stems from the fact that many school boards and superintendents met with teacher representatives and discussed issues such as salary raises, school procedures, health benefits, grievances, and some working conditions. Sometimes these informal discussions resulted in verbal agreements, sometimes they resulted in written documents, and sometimes they resulted in statements placed into the board policy manual; sometimes they were entered into the minutes of a board meeting. It should be remembered that, unlike in the private sector, most schools had employee organizations many years before anyone discussed collective bargaining. Most teachers and administrators joined the NEA at both the state and national levels, and established local organizations as well to further professional growth and to encourage social activities. Thus, when the push came for exclusive representation and collective bargaining, the teacher organization was already in place. The NEA had only to expel its administrative members, and it was ready to pressure legislatures.

Norwalk, Connecticut, is one of those claiming the earliest collective bargaining agreement for schools, back in 1946. This agreement followed a strike by the teachers' association, a group that was not affiliated with any state or national teachers' organization.[17]

Others say that the 1938 agreement between the Proviso Council of the West Suburban Teachers Union and their board was the first collective bargaining agreement. (The Proviso Township High School District is located in a suburban area west of Chicago.)

The best-known teacher unionization and collective bargaining agreement occurred in New York City. In 1961, the United Federation of Teachers won a victory as the exclusive bargaining agent for the city's teachers, replacing more than ninety existing bargaining unions. A formal agreement was signed a year later.[18]

At this same time, pressure was being applied to the NEA by some of its members to take a firmer stance in favor of collective bargaining for its members. For years, the NEA had been a respected professional organization for both teachers and administrators, and many of its members disliked the idea of its becoming another "union." Even today, while some local NEA affiliates think nothing of saying they are "teacher unions," others contend that they are "associations" or "organizations"—but not "unions."

In 1961, the NEA Representative Assembly passed resolutions on professional negotiations (they avoided the term "collective bargaining") and amended them at their next conference in 1962. They asked their member districts and boards to seek state legislation to establish the right of the teachers to negotiate collectively.[19]

In contrast, the National School Boards Association (NSBA) countered with a resolution at its 1963 national meeting, opposing state legislation on negotiations but supporting the right of teachers to discuss matters with the school board.[20]

During 1961–1965, the two dominant teacher organizations, the NEA and the AFT, battled each other to win representative elections. They opposed each other forty times in these elections, with the NEA victorious in twenty-six and the AFT in fourteen. However, the AFT won the large cities and won representation for three times the number of teachers as did the NEA in these forty elections.

In order to win representative elections, these two groups had to battle for the loyalty of the teachers. The NEA began to take a more militant stance on collective bargaining and on strikes in order to keep up with the AFT's positions. While differences still existed, the two organizations became more alike than before. Because of their similarity, the two organizations began to have discussions about merging. There were several unsuccessful attempts between 1969 and 1977, and eventually the NEA decided to restrict its membership to professional educational employees, while the AFT opened its membership to other workers, such as cafeteria workers, bus drivers, and even some outside of education, such as health care workers. In addition, the NEA strongly supported President Jimmy Carter's push for a cabinet-level Department of Education, while the AFT, under its late president Albert Shanker, opposed it. Merger talks resumed in the late 1990s, but the NEA delegates voted against it at their annual convention in 1998.[21]

Public education is the single largest employer in state and local government, with 5.1 million employees and expenditures of $400 billion in 1997.[22] In 1998, the NEA had 2.4 million members and the AFT had about 980,000. Despite some members' continued insistence that it is not a union, the NEA has been officially classified as a "union" since 1976 by the Bureau of Labor Statistics and the Internal Revenue Service.[23]

Finally, both teacher organizations, well trained and with good resources, were lobbying state legislatures for mandatory collective bargaining.

State Mandatory Collective Bargaining Laws

By 1960, only the state of Wisconsin had a mandatory negotiating law covering teachers; this law was not implemented until 1962, when the Wisconsin Employment Relations Board was established.[24] Basically the same provisions as those included in the Wisconsin law were passed into law in Connecticut, Michigan, and Massachusetts in 1965 and Rhode Island in 1966.[25]

More and more school districts abandoned the "meet and confer" style of discussion between the board/superintendent and the teacher representatives and began formal collective bargaining with written master contracts. Soon, more states began passing mandatory collective bargaining laws that required all their districts to negotiate.

In 1971, there were twenty-seven state collective bargaining laws for teachers, although very few of these early laws provided the right to strike. While there were similarities in these laws from state to state, there were also differences. Some laws applied to all public employees, some applied only to teachers, and some applied to teachers and all school administrators except the superintendent.[26]

Most of the state collective bargaining laws covered the following areas:

1. the right of public employees (or teachers) to organize;
2. the right of employees to be represented in collective bargaining by a representative of their choice;
3. a procedure to determine representation questions;
4. rules for the "duty to bargain" obligation for both employers and employee organizations;
5. a definition of ULPs and procedures for settling these;
6. procedures for settling impasses (mediation services, fact finding, and arbitration); and
7. the right to strike (in some states).

Even though some states prohibited strikes and other states had no state bargaining laws at all, strikes still occurred. During the 1960–1961 school year, there were three teacher strikes. In contrast, from 1968 to 1970, there were 180 strikes; there was a total of about 500 for the 1960s.

The first statewide teacher strike, and the first of six during the 1960s, occurred during 1963–1964 in Utah.[27] Most of these 1960s strikes resulted from (1) a recognition/representation question, (2) various grievances, and/or (3) negotiations.[28] The state bargaining laws sought to reduce some of the strikes by establishing provisions for these causes. The recognition/representation problem was addressed by establishing specific procedures for representative elections, with these procedures overseen by the state's employment relations board (similar to NLRB). The statutes tried to solve the grievance problem by insisting upon (in some states) a grievance procedure in the contract, possibly with advisory or binding arbitration as a final step in the grievance procedures. Finally, realizing that negotiations often ended in an impasse and possibly a strike, states set up timelines and procedures that required the use of mediators, fact finders, or arbitration at different points along the negotiations timeline.

By 1991, collective bargaining in the public schools was a reality in many districts across the nation. Of the fifty states, thirty-three had mandatory collective bargaining laws established by their legislatures.[29] In 1992, New Mexico passed a mandatory collective bargaining law, but this was rescinded in 1999. Thus, in 2002, the number of states with mandatory collective bargaining laws remained at thirty-three.[30] (Eight states prohibit collective bargaining, with six of these in the South: Arkansas, Louisiana, Mississippi, North Carolina, South Carolina, and Virginia. The other two states are in the West: Arizona and Colorado.)[31] Even in states that do not require bargaining, some districts choose to negotiate with their teachers on a formal basis. The negotiations process has gone from nonexistent to a process that only took a few hours at the end of each spring to cover the issues, to a process today that involves a great deal of time, money (directly or indirectly), and emotion. The remainder of this book is devoted to explaining the terms and issues noted in this chapter, discussing the roles in negotiations, giving suggestions for specific strategies at the bargaining table, dealing with strikes, and, finally, learning how to manage the contract.

SUMMARY

This chapter began with a historical perspective on private-sector bargaining, detailing the Ferguson Act, the Railway Labor Act, and the Wagner Labor Act, which established the NLRB. The provisions of the Taft–Harley Act were discussed along with the Landrum–Griffin Act. Following the perspective of the private sector, the chapter then discussed bargaining in the public sector, including executive orders by Presidents

Kennedy, Nixon, and Clinton. The roles of the NEA, NSBA, and AFT were discussed with respect to bargaining in the early years. The chapter concluded with a discussion of typical provisions of some state collective bargaining laws and teacher strikes in the early years. The next chapter gives a detailed description of a state collective bargaining law.

DISCUSSION QUESTIONS

1. What were the provisions of the Ferguson Act?
2. What is the function of the National Labor Relations Board?
3. What is the significance of each of the following:

   –Taft–Hartley Act?
   –Wagner Act?
   –Landrum–Griffin Act?

4. What are some "unfair labor practices" mentioned in the preceding acts?
5. What is the relevance of these acts from the 1940s and 1950s for today's public schools?
6. What were the three executive orders that were mentioned?
7. Discuss early "meet and confer" meetings prior to formal collective bargaining in schools.
8. What are the provisions of a typical state collective bargaining law?
9. What were the causes of most early school strikes?
10. What did the state collective bargaining laws contain to reduce strikes?

NOTES

1. J. R. Commons, "American Shoemakers, 1648–1895," in *Readings in Labor Economics and Labor Relations,* 4th ed., edited by R. L. Rowan, 57–59, (Homewood, Ill.: Irwin, 1980).

2. R. C. Kearney, *Labor Relations in the Public Sector* (New York: Dekker, 2001), 2.

3. Kearney, *Labor Relations,* 13.

4. Kearney, *Labor Relations,* 14.

5. D. Ziskind, *One Thousand Strikes of Government Employees* (New York: Columbia University Press, 1940).

6. William Manchester, *The Glory and the Dream* (Boston: Little, Brown, 1973), 1, 393.

7. John F. Lewis, R. Dean Jollay Jr., and Jonathan F. Buchter, *Ohio School Law* (Cleveland: Banks Baldwin, 1987), 241.

8. Robert C. O'Reilly, *Understanding Collective Bargaining in Education* (Metuchen, N.J.: Scarecrow, 1978), 8.

9. Alan E. Bent and T. Zane Reeves, *Collective Bargaining in the Public Sector* (Menlo Park, Calif.: Benjamin Cummings, 1978), 216.

10. Chapter 2 describes a state bargaining law in detail.

11. Bent and Reeves, *Collective Bargaining,* 217–18.

12. Kearney, *Labor Relations,* 47.

13. Lloyd W. Ashby, James E. McGinnis, and Thomas E. Persing, *Common Sense in Negotiations* (Danville, Ill.: Interstate, 1972), 2.

14. Ashby, McGinnis, and Persing, *Common Sense,* 4.

15. Kearney, *Labor Relations,* 53.

16. R. Tobias, "Federal Employee Unions and the Human Resource Management Functions," in *Handbook of Human Resources Management in Government,* edited by S. E. Condrey, 258–71 (San Francisco: Jossey-Bass, 1998).

17. T. M. Stinnett, Jack H. Kleinmann, and Martha L. Ware, *Professional Negotiation in Public Education* (New York: Macmillan, 1966), 7.

18. Ashby, McGinnis, and Persing, *Common Sense,* 2.

19. Stinnett, Kleinmann, and Ware, *Professional Negotiation,* 11.

20. Stinnett, Kleinmann, and Ware, *Professional Negotiation,* 12–13.

21. Kearney, *Labor Relations,* 38–39.

22. Kearney, *Labor Relations,* 37.

23. Kearney, *Labor Relations,* 38.

24. Ashby, McGinnis, and Persing, *Common Sense,* 6.

25. Kenneth O. Warner, ed., *Collective Bargaining in the Public Service: Theory and Practice* (Chicago: Public Personnel Association, 1967), 33.

26. Ashby, McGinnis, and Persing, *Common Sense,* 3.

27. Ashby, McGinnis, and Persing, *Common Sense,* 5.

28. Ashby, McGinnis, and Persing, *Common Sense,* 6.

29. Telephone conversation with NEA research, Washington, D.C., November 28, 1990.

30. Telephone conversation with NEA research, Washington, D.C., August 13, 2002.

31. Kearney, *Labor Relations,* 62–63.

2

STATE BARGAINING LAWS

As stated in the previous chapter, most of the states have adopted collective bargaining laws. While the individual provisions will vary from state to state, many aspects of these laws are similar. Having worked directly with three such state laws in the Midwest, this author can testify that there appear to be more similarities than differences among these laws. For this reason, this chapter examines one state bargaining law, recognizing that while it is not identical to laws of other states, it is similar enough to serve as an example.

A STATE COLLECTIVE BARGAINING LAW

Ohio, like many other states, resisted a state collective bargaining law for public employees. Twice, laws were passed and, twice, they were vetoed. Finally, in 1983, the legislature passed and the governor approved a collective bargaining law that went into effect on April 1, 1984.[1]

One of the most significant purposes of this law (and one typical of such state bargaining laws) was to establish a state employment relations board, fashioned after the National Labor Relations Board (NLRB) mentioned in chapter 1.

The state employment relations board is composed of three members, appointed by the governor and approved by the Senate. Most states that have a bargaining law have such a board, with the governor often appointing one Republican, one Democrat, and a third member from the governor's party. The members of the board often have labor relations backgrounds as attorneys, arbitrators, college professors, or politicians.

This board, in turn, hires a staff to help carry out the other provisions of the state bargaining law. In Ohio, the major functions of the board are as outlined next.

Conduct representative elections. The board must establish procedures so that teachers can vote on whether they want to be represented by an association and, if so, by which organization or group. The timing of the vote, the wording of the ballot, the voting procedures, and the counting of the votes are all responsibilities that the state board must oversee. When disputes or representative challenges arise, the state board must settle these debates.

Rule on unfair labor practices (ULPs). Chapter 3 examines this function in depth.

Establish a bureau of mediation. One of the "selling points" of state bargaining laws was that they would help settle contract disputes and prevent many strikes. Thus, one of the functions of the state board is to provide mediators to help resolve collective bargaining disputes before a strike occurs. Often, the state board establishes a time line, based on the number of days until a contract expires, for the successful completion of negotiations. Along that time line are points at which the state can intervene in the process to mediate the negotiations if sufficient progress is not being made.

In Ohio, there are points at fifty, forty-five, and thirty-one days before the contract expiration date when different provisions are activated to help the process (if necessary). The established helping procedures include mediation, arbitration, a citizen's council, and a fact-finding panel. In Ohio, the teachers can legally strike if they have proceeded through this process until the contract has expired and have given a written notice that they will strike. This notice must be given to their board of education and to the state employment relations board ten days prior to the strike. While the mediators may be used for other purposes (to see if they can settle a ULP charge, for example), their main purpose is to help both sides at the bargaining table come to an agreement.

Make recommendations to the legislature. The state board makes recommendations to the legislature for laws that, in its view, would improve collective bargaining in the state. This could involve the timetable just discussed, the scope of bargaining, ULPs, employee and employer rights, or anything else in the area of collective bargaining.

Train employers and employees in collective bargaining. The state recognizes that merely passing a law making collective bargaining mandatory does not make all the teacher and school board negotiators experts in the negotiation process. The state employment relations board was required to provide some training in collective bargaining and in the collective bargaining law. Needless to say, school district personnel also received help from other sources: the state school board association, the state superintendent association, and the state teacher association.

Conduct studies. The state employment relations board spends a lot of time gathering data on the status of employment, contracts, contract provisions, strikes, the use of its services, contract expiration dates, and other matters relating to collective bargaining. Studies of this data help the board make recommendations to the legislature and make reports to the legislature as they are requested.

Bargaining Units

A state bargaining law often defines what a **bargaining unit** is and who can be in it. For example, if a school board bargains with a group of teachers that has been duly elected as the representative of the teachers, those teachers constitute a bargaining unit. By contrast, in a nearby district due to historical reasons the school board may bargain with a group that represents the teachers, substitute teachers, *and* secretaries (although this is unlikely). This group is the bargaining unit in the second district since it was elected and agreed to by the teachers, secretaries, and substitutes. Another district might have three *different* bargaining units to represent these three classifications of employees. Again, the state employment relations board must establish procedures for electing the representatives of the employees. Once the teachers, for example, have elected their representative, the school board must negotiate only with this representative of the teachers. For this reason, this elected group is called the **exclusive bargaining agent** or **exclusive representative** of the teachers. This group continues to be the only representative of the teachers until a subsequent election brings in a new representative.

Most laws recognize that it would be unfair to have certain employees as members of a bargaining unit. For example, it would not be fair for the school board to bargain against a teachers' bargaining unit that included the assistant superintendent who was the negotiator for the board. Therefore, management is often excluded from such bargaining units, as are other "confidential" employees who work with the data used by the school board during negotiations. (However, it should be pointed out that some states allow some management positions to negotiate as a separate group: the principals or the central-office staff, for example.)

Lewis and Spim state that confidential employees include those who "work in the personnel office of an employer and deal with information used by the employer in collective bargaining, or employees who work in a close continuing relationship with public officers or representatives directly participating in collective bargaining on behalf of the employer."[2] However, an employee in the personnel office who does not deal with collective bargaining matters would not be considered as "confidential." Defining who "management" is may cause problems, especially when dealing with positions that have both management and non-management responsibilities: department chairpersons or supervisors, athletic directors, and head teachers. The state employment relations board usually insists that "management" means those who have the authority to hire, transfer, suspend, lay off, recall, promote, discharge, assign, reward, and discipline. Often, a dispute over whether Athletic Director Jones or Math Department Chair Smith is or is not in the bargaining unit has to be negotiated between the school board and the bargaining unit's exclusive representative or ultimately decided by the state employment relations board. In Ohio, "department chairmen" and "consulting teachers" are expressly excluded from the concept of "management" under the collective bargaining act, even if they have been given the appropriate authority.[3]

Even if employees have some supervisory responsibilities, they will not automatically be classified as management or supervisors for purposes of collective bargaining. For example, head custodians who supervise beginning custodians are not "supervisors" unless they have authority to recommend employment actions and are held accountable for the work of the other custodians.[4]

EXAMPLE: The State Employment Relations Board (SERB) in Ohio heard a case in which a supervisor stated that two lower management employees had authority to discipline their subordinates either orally or in writing. Also, these managers said that the supervisor had advised them about when and in what manner they should discipline the workers. However, they had never exercised this authority independently. In addition, the managers sometimes interviewed candidates for employment and made recommendations to the supervisor who held independent interviews of the candidates. Finally, these managers made evaluations of the workers, but these evaluations could be changed by the supervisor. As a result, the SERB found that the managers did not have independent authority and that independent authority/judgment was necessary for someone to be considered a supervisor under the collective bargaining law.[5]

Employee Rights

As stated before, the state legislatures mimicked the national picture by establishing state employment relations boards similar to the NLRB and by passing state collective bargaining laws that had sections very much like parts of the Taft–Hartley Act of 1947. Some of the employee rights mentioned in the Ohio Collective Bargaining Law are listed next. They should appear similar to statements made in the labor laws of the 1940s (mentioned in chapter 1).

1. Employees can join or refrain from joining an employee organization of their own choosing. Implicit in this right may be the right of employees to distribute information related to their right to organize, unless it interferes with the job performance.[6] Private-sector decisions have affirmed the right of the employer to restrict such distribution to break periods, mealtimes, or other nonwork periods.[7] However, any such rule concerning distribution cannot be discriminatory. For example, if employees who engage in union solicitation are disciplined, but employees who solicit for other purposes are not disciplined, it is a case of unlawful discrimination.[8] An exception was made by the NLRB when it affirmed that an employer could allow charitable solicitations and prohibit other solicitations by employees.[9]

Because this provision also provides that employees can refrain from joining an organization, the employer is allowed to campaign actively against a union.[10] However, the employer must be careful in conducting this campaign. In the private sector, management has been allowed to give speeches to employees on company time without the union being given similar response time.[11] However, these speeches have not been allowed within twenty-four hours of an election.[12] An employer may distribute literature and give its personal view of a union, but the employer cannot threaten harm if a union is victorious in the election or promise a benefit if the union is defeated.[13] Likewise, it has been considered to be coercive if the employer calls employees into the employer's office to discuss the union, while it is permissible to conduct the identical conversation at the work station of the employee.[14]

2. Employees can engage in other activities for the purpose of collective bargaining or other mutual aid and protection. Since the terms in this section have not been defined by the law, their definitions will have to be decided by cases received by the state employment relations board. In the private sector, such concerted activity has been defined to include any activity that has some relation to group action and is in the interest of the employees.[15] Three factors have been used in labor law to determine whether action is considered concerted action: (1) whether the employee acted alone and without union advice or sought to involve and inform other employees; (2) the degree of union involvement and concern with the dispute; and (3) whether the subject of the complaint has at least an arguable basis in the collective bargaining agreement.[16]

EXAMPLE: Examples of actions for mutual aid and protection are writing a letter complaining of sanitary conditions on behalf of other employees,[17] refusing in the course of employment to cross a picket line located in another employer's place of business,[18] and issuing letters to the public concerning collective bargaining.[19] Lewis and Spim state that "one of the most significant aspects of concerted activity is the role of a union representative in disciplinary interviews."[20] The Supreme Court held that an employee's insistence upon union representation at an employer's investigation interview, if the employee reasonably believes the interview might result in disciplinary action against him, is protected concerted activity.[21]

3. Employees can be represented by an employee organization. To prevent elections every few months by rival organizations (and to preserve some labor peace), there can be no representative election during the term of a valid contract between the employer and the exclusive representative. This is known as the "contract bar."[22] When an employee organization is elected to represent the employees, it remains the exclusive representative for at least one year. This is called the "election bar."[23] An exception to these "bars" can be made by the state employment relations board if the union becomes defunct or if there is so much intraunion conflict that only an election can establish union order.[24]

4. Employees can bargain collectively with their employer to determine wages, hours, terms, and other conditions of employment and enter into agreements. This employee right to "bargain collectively" is the essence of the whole bargaining law. The public employer has a duty to bargain collectively with the elected, exclusive bargaining representative of the employees. Both sides must negotiate "in good faith" at reasonable times and places and intend to reach an agreement. While the law states that it does not require either side to agree to a proposal or make any concessions, any party that refuses to do so would probably be accused of not "negotiating in good faith." Also, when it states "at reasonable times and places," it means that both sides should agree upon these times and places—neither side can insist on a time or place to negotiate. In reality, "time and place" are negotiable, too.

In addition to the preceding, the employer must provide to the union information relevant to negotiations: the budget, financial records and reports, public information furnished to the school board, actual employee salaries, schedules, and fringe benefits, along with other documents.[25]

5. Employees can present grievances to their employer and have them adjusted, as long as the adjustment is consistent with the collective bargaining agreement and the bargaining representative has the opportunity to be present at the adjustment. Not all states allow individual employees to present grievances as stated in this provision. Note, however, that the employee cannot present the grievance without the union representative being allowed to attend the meeting in which the decision/adjustment/remedy is made with the employee. It is not clear whether the union representative is also allowed to be present at all earlier stages of the grievance process.[26]

The Contract

The state bargaining law also tells what must be contained in the final bargaining agreement. These provisions will vary from state to state, but Ohio's provisions provide a good example.

It must be in writing. Oral agreements are a thing of the past. This is a formal document that is usually duplicated for both employees and management. (Today's word processing makes the job of changing the language sections easy.)

It cannot be for more than three years. A contract can be a one-year agreement or a multiyear contract covering either two or three years. Some contracts may cover all language sections for two or three years with a provision to discuss salary items each year (see "Consider a reopener," chapter 6).

It must contain a grievance procedure. The Ohio law requires some type of grievance procedure. It allows binding arbitration, something favored by the employee organization, but the law does not require it in the procedure. (Chapter 10 details grievances.)

It must contain a dues checkoff provision. This is a valuable provision for the union. Without this provision in the contract (either by law or by negotiated agreement), the union would have to contact each member and ask him or her to write a check for union dues, which is now typically several hundred dollars a year. This provision lets the member pay the dues by payroll deduction, probably over an extended period.

It must contain substantial terms and conditions of employment. This does not seem to pose a problem, as most contracts have become very lengthy documents covering many aspects of "terms and conditions of employment."

It must be signed by each side. Who actually signs is determined by each side. Of course, the agreement should be ratified by a vote of each party.

It must have an expiration date. This is an exact date: August 27, 2008, for example. Remember that all the provisions in the law dealing with mediation, arbitration, fact-finding, and strikes are based on a time line with this expiration date as the base.

It supersedes state law. Sometimes it does. In the area of terms and conditions of employment, the contract supersedes state law. If the state law says a teacher gets ten sick days and the contract says a teacher receives twelve days, the contract takes precedence. However, when dealing with educational requirements such as certification requirements, the state law supersedes the contract.

It allows, but does not require, agency shop. The collective bargaining agreement may require, as a condition of employment, that employees in the bargaining unit who have not chosen to join the union as members pay a "fair-share" fee. The Ohio bargaining law does not allow **union shop**, in which an employee must join and retain membership in the union. It does allow **agency shop**, in which the employee pays a fair-share fee but does not join the union.

The fair-share fee, as determined by the union, is usually similar to the union dues. The union philosophy is that all members of the bargaining unit receive services such as collective bargaining, the handling of grievances, and other representation and should pay for these services regardless of whether they join the union or not. The amount of money in the dues that is available for partisan political purposes or ideological causes not related to the collective bargaining function is excluded from the fair-share amount paid by nonmembers. There is also a provision in the law for those people who have religious objections to contributing such a fair share. Four states require a fair-share provision in the contract, fifteen states allow teacher unions to negotiate it, and thirty-one states prohibit fair share (or prohibit collective bargaining in general).[27]

It should be remembered that agency shop is permitted by the law, not required. If the school board does not wish to agree to agency shop in the contract, it does not have to do so.

The Scope of Bargaining

The Ohio law specifies **mandatory** areas of bargaining: all matters pertaining to wages, hours, terms and other conditions of employment, and modification or deletion of existing provisions of the collective bargaining agreement. These areas, which must be negotiated, have been interpreted fairly liberally in most states, meaning that the board often has to negotiate (but not necessarily agree with) areas that it wishes it could avoid. The language in the Ohio law differs from that of other states and from the NLRB definition. Notice that the Ohio law states "all matters pertaining" to wages and so on. Also, unlike most laws, which use "and" between the words "hours" and "terms," Ohio uses the word "or." Both of these differences make the Ohio law more liberal in interpretation than the laws of some other states. In some states, such as Ohio, areas already in the contract are subject to negotiation by both sides. However, this is not true everywhere. The term "wages" is interpreted to include salaries, hourly rates, fringe benefits such as health insurance, sick leave, personal leave, overtime pay, pay for supplementary duties like coaching, and employer's contribution to pension plans.[28] The term "hours" includes the length of the employee work day and the number of days in the workweek and work year.

Permissive areas of negotiations are those that may be negotiated: board policy, supervision of employees, hiring or discharging employees, the overall budget, utilization of technology, organizational structure, the scheduling of employees, and other areas often associated with management. Boards should be cautious about negotiating away their management prerogatives. To complicate the concept that management rights arc a permissive subject of negotiations, the law states that the employer is required to bargain on management rights if they "affect" wages, hours, terms, and conditions of employment. Obviously, this sentence expands the topics to be bargained and increases the possibility for cases to be decided by the state employment relations board in interpreting this sentence. Lewis and Spim discuss this problem by stating that virtually all management decisions affect employees in some way. A decision to buy a bus has an effect on a bus driver's job. However, this would be considered a management right, not subject to negotiations since it primarily concerns the school board's management of the school district, not the employer–employee relationship. However, to make a management decision to hire a private company to provide bus drivers and lay off the district's drivers would impact the employer–employee relationship and would be the subject of bargaining (assuming the bus drivers were unionized).[29] Examples of items that concern employees but are usually considered management areas (not subject to negotiations) are the decision to have a three-year high school instead of a four-year school, the decision to close a school, and decisions regarding curriculum. Of course, the school board must bargain the effects of these decisions: the transfer or laying off of employees due to a new structure or the closing of a school or a new curriculum.[30]

Prohibited areas are those that *cannot* be negotiated. State minimum regulations on teacher certification and teacher certification examinations are two areas that cannot be negotiated. However, there are very few areas affecting teachers that cannot be the subject of negotiations.

During the term of the contract, an employer can act unilaterally on a permissive subject of negotiations, but not on a mandatory area of bargaining, which would be considered an unfair labor practice. For example, unless the contract specifies otherwise, the board and administration may hire and discharge employees on their own. However, they cannot change salaries, even to raise them, without negotiating them with the union.

As stated earlier, the Ohio bargaining law is only one example of a state bargaining law, but its provisions are very similar to those in other states that have such laws. Each state's law has its own peculiarities—Indiana has a required "discussion" section detailing what must be discussed with the union before action is taken—but most state laws contain provisions dealing with a state labor board, employee rights, the duty to bargain collectively, the contractual provisions, and the scope of bargaining as shown in the example in this chapter. The next chapter discusses a final point of the state's collective bargaining law: ULPs.

SUMMARY

This chapter discussed the Ohio Collective Bargaining Law as an example of a typical state bargaining law for teachers. The state employment relations board and its functions were detailed. The concepts of a bargaining unit and an exclusive bargaining agent were explained. Next, the chapter enumerated the rights of employees under the Act and discussed the duty to bargain collectively. The chapter concluded with a discussion of the provisions of a contract and the scope of bargaining. One of the provisions of a state collective bargaining law is unfair labor practices, the subject of the next chapter.

DISCUSSION QUESTIONS

1. What are some of the similarities between a state collective bargaining law for public employees and the laws for private employees of the 1940s and 1950s?
2. What are typical functions of the state employment relations board?
3. What are representative elections?
4. What is a bargaining unit?
5. How is "management" usually defined?
6. What are some employee rights present in a typical state collective bargaining law?
7. What does "duty to bargain collectively" involve?
8. Why is a dues checkoff provision useful to a union?
9. When can a school contract supersede a state law?
10. Contrast union shop and agency shop.
11. What is a "fair-share" fee?
12. Differentiate between mandatory, permissive, and prohibited areas of bargaining.

NOTES

1. Ohio Revised Code, Chapter 4117: Public Employees' Collective Bargaining.

2. John F. Lewis and Steven Spim, *Ohio Collective Bargaining Law* (Cleveland: Banks–Baldwin Law, 1983), 30.

3. Lewis and Spim, *Ohio Collective Bargaining Law*, 31.

4. Lewis and Spim, *Ohio Collective Bargaining Law*, 31.

5. SERB 89-028, *District 925, Service Employees International Union v. University of Cincinnati* (1989).

6. *Republic Aviation Corp. v. NLRB*, 324 US 793, 65 SCt 982, 89 LEd 1372 (1945).

7. *TWR Bearing Div.*, 257 NLRB 442 (1981).

8. Lewis and Spim, *Ohio Collective Bargaining Law*, 39.

9. Lewis and Spim, *Ohio Collective Bargaining Law*, 40.

10. Lewis and Spim, *Ohio Collective Bargaining Law*, 40.

11. *NLRB v. United Steelworkers of America*, 357 US 357, 78 SO 1268, 2 LEd (2d) 1383 (1958).

12. *Peerless Plywood*, 107 NLRB 427 (1954).

13. Lewis and Spim, *Ohio Collective Bargaining Law*, 40.

14. Bowmar Instrument Corp., 124 NLRB 1 (1959), and Eastern Metal Products Corp., 114 NLRB 239 (1955).

15. *Mushroom Transportation Co. v. NLRB*, 330 F(2d) 683 (3rd Cir 1964).

16. Lewis and Spim, *Ohio Collective Bargaining Law*, 41–42.

17. *Wall's Mfg. Co. v. NLRB*, 321 F(2d) 753 (DC Cir 1963).

18. *Redwing Carriers, Inc.*, 137 NLRB (1962).

19. *City of West Palm Beach v. Palm Beach City Police*, 3 CCH Public Barg, 1980.

20. Lewis and Spim, *Ohio Collective Bargaining Law*, 42.

21. *NLRB v. J. Weingarten, Inc.*, 420 US 251, 95 SO 959, 43 LEd (2d) 171 (1975).

22. Lewis and Spim, *Ohio Collective Bargaining Law*, 48.

23. SERB 89-035, December 29, 1989.

24. Lewis and Spim, *Ohio Collective Bargaining Law*, 48–49.

25. *NLRB v. Truitt Mtg. Co.*, 351 US 149 (1956).

26. Lewis and Spim, *Ohio Collective Bargaining Law*, 41.

27. Myron Lieberman, *Unions: How They Sabotage Educational Reform and Why* (San Francisco: Encounter, 2000), 182.

28. Lieberman, *Unions*, 60.

29. Lieberman, *Unions*, 61.

30. Lieberman, *Unions*, 62.

3

UNFAIR LABOR PRACTICES

Chapter 1 noted that the National Labor Relations Board (NLRB), established by the Wagner Act in 1935, outlawed unfair labor practices by employers against employees and employee unions in the private sector. The Taft–Hartley Act of 1947 placed restrictions on both employee organizations and employers. Some of the restrictions were listed in that chapter.

Chapter 2 enumerated some employee rights in a state bargaining law for public employees. These were similar to the employee rights recognized in the private sector.

The "unfair labor practice" (ULP) concept from the private sector was carried over to the public sector to reflect prohibited actions against the rights of employees and employers in the public sector. Just as the state employment relations board (for the public sector) is similar to the NLRB, and the rights of employees in the public sector are similar to those of employees in the private sector, unfair labor practices are similar in both sectors. This chapter examines the concept of unfair labor practices by both employers and unions.

UNFAIR LABOR PRACTICES BY THE EMPLOYER

Following are examples of actions that would be considered prohibited in a state that has a typical collective bargaining law for public employees. In other words, it would constitute an unfair labor practice for the employer to do the following:

1. To interfere with, restrain, or coerce employees in exercising their rights or in the selection of their representative for collective bargaining. The employer (school board) must allow the employees (teachers, for example) to hold a fair election that will decide who the exclusive bargaining representative will be for those employees. The board cannot interfere in this process or try to coerce employees to vote a certain way in the election. The employees have the right to pick their representative without outside interference.

EXAMPLE: The following have been found to be unlawful:

- The surveillance of union members or union meetings by hired spies, supervisors, or other employees reporting to managers *(Consolidated Edison v. NLRB)*[1]
- Coercive interrogation of employees about their union affiliation or union activities *(NLRB v. Heck's)*[2]
- Blacklisting union members by circulating their names to other employers *(NLRB v. Waumbec Mills)*[3]
- Physical intimidation of union members *(Regal Shirt Co. v. NLRB)*[4]
- Promising or actually granting salary increases or other fringe benefits to discourage union activities *(Warren Paint & Color Co. v. NLRB)*[5]
- Threatening to discipline employees, eliminate benefits, withhold future benefits, or take reprisals against employees if they engage in union activities *(Parkwood Homes v. NLRB)*[6]

Some specific examples of labor practices that were found to be unfair are outlined next:

- A State Employment Relations Board (SERB) decision. A school board sent letters to school employees stating that health insurance benefits had been cancelled, implemented its final negotiations offer, and transferred employees following a strike. The letter that was sent to employees contained a summary of negotiations. The letter also contained the superintendent's comments. These comments stated that the union might not present the board's last bargaining offer to the employees and that the employees should not allow themselves to be led to a strike. Also, the superintendent invited the members to contact the administration directly to discuss this information. A second letter was sent, mentioning that the insurance had been cancelled the first day of the strike. The school board was found to be guilty of an unfair labor practice.[7]

- A SERB decision. A school employees' union filed a petition for voluntary recognition in response to which a petition for representative election was filed by the school board. A maintenance supervisor who had been discussing building maintenance with an employee remarked about the upcoming election, "Who was for the union at the high school?" This question was found to be coercive and in violation of this section of the law and to have tainted the election, necessitating a new election. Another employer's remark that employees would not be able to communicate directly with the employer if a union was certified was also coercive and prevented a free election.[8]

- A SERB decision. In some states, individual employees are given the right to file grievances on their own but must allow the union to be present at the adjustment of those grievances. In other states, employees must file through the union, not on their own. In this case, a public employer agreed to hear a grievance of an employee and gave every indication that it understood that the matter was being handled by and through a union as the exclusive representative. However, the employer proceeded to reach a settlement with the employee without notifying the union of the settlement. This was an unfair labor practice, even if the employee had the right to file on his own.[9]

- A SERB decision. A principal asked three employees not to apply for an open secretarial position. The SERB board found that this action by the principal interfered with the employee's rights in their collective bargaining agreement.[10]

2. To interfere with the administration of the employee organization. Once the employees have elected their representative, they have the right to select their own officers to run the employee organization as they see fit. The employer cannot interfere by putting pressure on employees to select certain officers, for example. This section also allows an

employer to permit employees to confer with the employer during working hours without loss of time or pay, to allow the union representative to
use the employer's facilities for membership or other meetings, and to allow the union to use the internal mail system. However, the employer
should note that the language used here is permissive, not mandatory.[11]

EXAMPLE: It is an unfair labor practice for the employer to attempt
to establish a "company union," that is, one that it controls (*California
School Employees Assoc. v. Tustin Unified School District*).[12] The employer may not:

- emphasize favoritism for one labor organization over another;[13]
- interfere in some way with the internal operations of the employees'
  exclusive representative.[14]

3. To discriminate in hiring or granting tenure. The school
board/administration cannot make decisions on hiring or tenure on the
basis of employee organizational rights. For example, an administrator
cannot hire a teacher with the agreement that he or she would not join
the union. Likewise, the administration cannot tell a teacher that tenure
will be based on whether the teacher joins the union or participates in
union activities or negotiations. It would be an unfair labor practice to
do so. (An exception: Since the school board must enforce agency shop
if it is a part of the contract, the board must dismiss anyone who does
not pay a fair-share fee.)

EXAMPLE: The most typical example of a violation of this section is
one of discriminatory discipline. While the employer has a managerial
right to discipline employees, it is an unfair labor practice to use this discipline as a means of interfering with the employee's protected rights.[15]

4. To discriminate against an employee who files charges. An
employee has the right to file grievances and unfair labor practice
charges against the employer without being subjected to discrimination
by the employer in terms of promotion, tenure, retention, and other
conditions of employment.

EXAMPLE: A SERB decision. An unfair labor practice was found when
a school district denied tenure to a teacher who had filed an earlier grievance. The superintendent stated that the teacher had failed to improve
performance in the two years following the grievance. However, the su-

perintendent disregarded the principal's evaluation, which recommended tenure for the teacher and showed that the teacher's deficiencies had been corrected. The SERB thought that the only intervening event that could have changed the employer's original intent to award improvement with tenure was the grievance filed by the teacher, which resulted in an arbitration award critical of the employer.[16]

5. To refuse to bargain collectively. The employer must bargain collectively with the exclusive bargaining representative. As stated in the last chapter, the employer must bargain "in good faith" at reasonable times and places and must intend to reach an agreement. The employer cannot unilaterally change wages, benefits, or working conditions without bargaining with the exclusive bargaining representative. In *NLRB v. Katz,* the employer, during negotiations and without any notification to the exclusive representative, unilaterally announced wage increases and a change in its sick leave policy. The Supreme Court found that this unilateral action was a refusal to bargain, even though the action was of benefit to the employees and may not have been done in bad faith.[17] Many unfair labor practices are filed against employers because they are charged with refusing to bargain in good faith or with taking unilateral action to change working conditions.

When a state board or court examines this section for a possible violation, they look at the employer's conduct as a whole at the bargaining table to determine whether the employer is bargaining in good faith. This conduct must reflect a willingness to present proposals, articulate supporting reasons, listen to and evaluate the union proposals and reasons, and search for common ground so that a written contract can eventually be developed.[18]

EXAMPLE: It was found to be unlawful for an employer to make a direct proposal to employees exceeding the terms offered to the union at the bargaining table *(NLRB v. J. H. Bonck Co.).*[19] At the same time, the NLRB has held that an employer can tell employees the status of negotiations, proposals previously made, and why a breakdown has occurred, as long as the employer does so in noncoercive terms *(Proctor & Gamble v. NLRB).*[20] Some specific cases are presented next.

- A SERB decision. A school employees' union filed an unfair labor practice, stating that the school board had refused to bargain.

There were a number of union proposals presented to the school board, to which the board responded by presenting their counter-proposals and stating, "Take it or leave it." The board's responses were considered as refusals to bargain in good faith.[21]

- A SERB decision. An employer refused to deduct union dues from employee paychecks, even though the contract stated that it should be done if a form is "signed individually and voluntarily" by the employee and is then "presented to the employer by the employee." In this case, the employer refused to honor the forms presented to him by the union on the ground that he did not know the forms had been signed voluntarily and did not see the forms signed. SERB found an unfair labor practice on the part of the employer because the employer had unilaterally imposed a condition not in the contract and infringed upon his employees' right to bargain collectively. The employer was ordered to pay the uncollected dues to the union from its own funds.[22]

- A SERB decision. In another unfair practice, the employer (who, interestingly, was the Office of Collective Bargaining for the State of Ohio) increased the health insurance premiums for the employees, selecting this option from several given to it from a joint employer–union committee. The employer's imposition of this increase without bargaining about which option to select or the amount of the increase was an unfair labor practice.[23]

- A SERB decision. A board of education tried to comply with a state regulation that required that its elementary librarians be supervised by a librarian with a certificate. To come into compliance, the board of education offered the head high school librarian a supplemental contract (used for all extra duties such as coaching) to supervise the elementary school librarians. This contract called for additional compensation and responsibility for the high school librarian. Since the board did not bargain this additional compensation for a member of the bargaining unit, it was guilty of refusing to bargain with the union. The employer must give notice to the union of its intention to make such a change. It cannot bargain after the fact to avoid the unfair practice. During the time it took for the unfair practice hearing to be heard and concluded, the board chose not to renew this supplemental contract since it felt it should find out the outcome of the case before proceeding to renew the contract. The board was found to have committed a second unfair practice because it discriminated against an employee on the basis of protected activity.[24]

- A final SERB decision. A school board distributed a negotiations report to bargaining unit members. The report indicated the proposals and counterproposals made by each side without any editorial comment and summarized the bargaining positions taken by the two sides up to the declaration of impasse. During the meeting of the union members, the union's strategy was attacked by members as a result of information gained from this negotiations report. Despite the board's insistence that it had the right to communicate the status of negotiations and the terms of its final offer to its employees, the SERB found that the board had violated the bargaining law because the report damaged the relationship of the exclusive representative with the members it represented and placed the union in a defensive bargaining position.[25]

6. To establish a pattern of repeated failure to timely process grievances and arbitrations. Grievance procedures usually contain a timetable that describes when grievances must be answered by the administration. If the administration repeatedly fails to meet this timetable, they can be accused of committing an unfair labor practice.

EXAMPLE: A SERB case with a positive decision for management. An employer received four grievances within a short period. All four of the grievances were processed in a timely manner at steps one and two of the grievance process but were backlogged at step three. Three of the four grievances had a step-three meeting within three and one-half months of the step-two denial and the fourth had a delay of one year. SERB found that the employer did not anticipate the volume of grievances that were filed by the new bargaining unit, and when it became clear that the problem was not a short-term one, the employer added staff to deal with the workload. The excessive delay in the one case (the fourth grievance) did not rise to the level of an unfair practice.[26]

7. To lock out employees in order to force them to agree to the employer's terms. This means that the school board, unlike some private employers, cannot lock out their employees in order to put pressure on them to accept the board's position at the bargaining table. Of course, the board can close the schools in the event of a teacher strike, although teachers have the right to report to work while some of the other teachers remain on strike.

EXAMPLE: In some states that allow school strikes under certain conditions (e.g., prior notice, impasse), there has been some confusion when teachers stage "partial" strikes. In one SERB case involving such a strike, the school board was notified by the teachers that they intended to "abstain in part from the full, faithful and proper performance of the duties of employment." This abstention involved times during the school day when the teachers would strike at different schools in the district. At all other times during the school day, the teachers pursued their regular assignments. The school board felt that this intermittent strike violated the state law. As a result, the board cancelled all extracurricular activities of striking teachers, reduced the paychecks of the striking teachers, and refused to compensate teachers subpoenaed to an unauthorized strike hearing. The teachers, for their part, felt that the board had not paid them for the time worked. SERB found that the board locked out or otherwise prevented employees from performing their regularly assigned duties because the board wanted to bring pressure on the employees or on the union to compromise or capitulate to the employer's terms at the bargaining table.[27]

8. To cause or attempt to cause an employee organization to commit an unfair labor practice. The employer cannot put the employee organization in such a position that it must commit an unfair labor practice.

UNFAIR LABOR PRACTICES BY THE UNION

Typically, a state bargaining law will also have prohibitions against the employee organization. For example, it is an unfair labor practice for the union to do the following:

1. To coerce employees in the exercise of their rights. Remember that employees have the right to refrain from joining a union or engaging in its activities, as well as the right to join and participate. Thus, the union must allow the employees to exercise those rights, to choose their exclusive representative (which may mean that a different union takes power), and to file grievances, whether or not the employee is a member of the union or the union agrees with the grievance. (This is not allowed in all states.)

EXAMPLE: The most common example of union restraint or coercion is violence, intimidation, or reprisals against the employees who refuse to join the union (*Service Employees International* case).[28] Other examples of coercion are as follows:

- The Supreme Court has allowed unions to fine members who cross a picket line in order to work because union solidarity is essential in a strike. However, it is unlawful for a union to use union discipline because members refuse to violate the law or the labor contract when instructed to do so by the union (*NLRB v. Allis-Chalmers, Bricklayers Local 2 v. NLRB*).[29]
- Discipline by the union can only be applied to union members, not to members of the bargaining unit who are not union members and only pay a fair-share fee.[30]
- Just as employers are not allowed to blacklist union members with other employers, unions are not allowed to blacklist employees with other unions (*Teamsters Local 1040 v. NLRB*).[31]

2. To cause or attempt to cause an employer to commit an unfair labor practice.

3. To refuse to bargain collectively with the employer. This and the previous item are, of course, parallel to the prohibitions discussed in the previous section.

EXAMPLE: A union cannot attempt to bargain on behalf of employees (e.g., supervisors) who are outside the bargaining unit (*NLRB v. Retail Clerks International*).[32] Also, a union cannot dictate to the employer who the employer must have at the bargaining table to represent management. (*Teamsters Local 70 v. NLRB*)[33]

4. To fail to represent fairly all employees in the bargaining unit. Sometimes the administration cannot understand why the union is backing an employee in a particular situation. Unions are obligated by law to represent all the employees, not just union members. In some situations, the administration may detect that the union's pressure, tactics, time, and money may not be devoted as strongly to some topics as they are to others. While the union has to represent everyone fairly, it still may choose to fight harder on some issues than on others.

EXAMPLE: The union can be found guilty of an unfair practice if it processes a grievance in a perfunctory manner. The Supreme Court found this to be the case in *Vaca v. Sipes*. A union does not fulfill its duty to all employees in the bargaining unit if it is "arbitrary, discriminatory, or in bad faith" in its conduct toward the employee. It may not ignore a meritorious grievance or process it in a perfunctory manner. However, the union does have the right to withdraw the grievance or settle the grievance short of arbitration without breaching the duty of the fair representation.[34]

- A SERB decision. A union tried to publicize a grievance by contacting the media. As a result, there were numerous television and radio reports, and newspaper articles. African-American and Jewish union members were asked to present testimony on the grievance by the union. However, no African-American or Jewish members showed up to give testimony for the union, but union members, both African-American and Caucasian, gave testimony that the union was not representing the interests of the bargaining unit members and that a majority of members opposed this grievance. The employer brought an unfair labor practice grievance against the union for failure to represent all members of the bargaining unit. The SERB found for the union because the employer lacked standing since there was no evidence of harm to the employer, press coverage was not harm to the employer in this case, and the union was required to enforce the contract even if a majority of its members failed to back the enforcement. The union's duty to fairly represent all employees should not be confused with majority rule.[35]

5. To violate prohibitions regarding picketing, strikes, and other actions. These will differ from state to state. To use Ohio as an example again, unions are prohibited from boycotting or picketing against the employer, the business of a board member, or the residence of a board member or encouraging employees to engage in an illegal strike. It is also an unfair labor practice (in Ohio) to picket or strike unless a ten-day notice is given to the state employment relations board and the school board specifying the date and time that the action will begin. If the SERB believes that an unauthorized strike exists, the school board can remove or suspend employees one day after they have been notified that this will happen if they continue with the strike. In 2001, 782 Unfair Labor Practices were filed with Ohio's SERB. Of these, 574 were alleged employer violations and 208 were alleged violations by the employee organization.[36]

PROCEDURES FOR AN UNFAIR LABOR PRACTICE

Typically, like grievances, the party filing an unfair labor practice charge has a time limit (perhaps ninety days) in which to file the charge. When the state employment relations board receives the charge, it conducts an investigation to see if there is probable cause. Sometimes the investigating official will bring both sides together during this investigation and see if there is any possibility of solving the problem without pursuing the ULP charge. If the investigator finds that there is no cause for a ULP, the charge is dismissed. If there is probable cause, a hearing is scheduled to let both parties present their sides of the issue.

The hearing is like a small, informal trial. The hearing officer assigned by the state employment relations board meets with both parties, often at the school site. The officer listens to the arguments of both sides, reads their documents, hears the testimony of the witnesses, and renders a decision on the ULP charge (or files a recommendation with the state employment relations board).

Some of the typical decisions are:

1. *A cease and desist order.* If, for example, the school board/ administration has been found "guilty" of committing a ULP, the state employment relations board may issue a cease and desist order. This informs the school board that it has committed a ULP and that it must stop the practice that resulted in this charge being filed. There is the implication that if the school board continues the practice, it will receive a more severe penalty in the future.
2. *A dismissal.* Even if probable cause is found during the investigation, the testimony and evidence may convince the hearing officer that the charge is without merit and should be dismissed.

3. *The reinstatement of employees.* Sometimes the decision can result in the ordering of reinstatement of employees with or without back pay. This decision can have important personnel and financial consequences.

4. *The restoration of the status quo.* If the school board, for example, unilaterally institutes a change in working conditions that should have been bargained with the exclusive representative, the state employment relations board may order that conditions be returned to the way they were before any change was made (the status quo). This may also be accompanied by a cease and desist order to avoid such unilateral actions in the future.

Decisions of the state employment relations board are subject to appeal to the courts.

SUMMARY

This chapter began with examples of actions that would constitute ULPs by the employer. These included such actions as interfering with the selection of the representative for collective bargaining or with the administration of the employee organization, discriminating against employees for union activities, and refusing to bargain collectively. This was followed by a list of activities that would be considered ULPs by the union: coercing employees in the exercise of their rights, refusing to bargain collectively, and failing to represent the employees. The chapter concluded by giving a description of the procedures for a ULP, including hearings on unfair practices, and listing some of the typical decisions that might result from such a hearing. The next three chapters discuss actual negotiations, beginning with the roles people play in negotiations.

DISCUSSION QUESTIONS

1. Discuss some unfair labor practices by an employer; by an employee organization.
2. In what way can an employer refuse to bargain collectively?

3. What typically happens when an unfair labor practice is filed with the state?
4. Describe the unfair labor practice hearing.
5. What are some typical decisions resulting from an unfair labor practice hearing?
6. When is the restoration of the status quo usually ordered?
7. What is a cease and desist order?
8. What does it mean to negotiate "in good faith"?
9. What can be wrong with the school administration taking unilateral action?
10. How can a union commit an unfair labor practice dealing with employee rights?

NOTES

Many of the following cases (except the SERB ones) are cited in John F. Lewis and Steven Spim, *Ohio Collective Bargaining Law* (Cleveland: Banks-Baldwin Law, 1983), or can be found in the original citations given next.

1. *Consolidated Edison Co. v. NLRB*, 305 US 197, 59 SO 206, 83 LEd 126 (1938).
2. *NLRB v. Heck's, Inc.*, 386 F(2d) 317 (4th Cir 1967).
3. *NLRB v. Waumbec Mills*, 144 F(2d) 226 (1st Cir 1940)
4. *Regal Shirt Co.* 4 NLRB 567 (1937).
5. *Warren Paint & Color Co.* 142 NLRB 494 (1963).
6. *Parkwood Homes, Inc.* 170 NLRB 1451 (1968).
7. SERB 90-003, *Ohio Assoc. of Public School Employees v. Vandalia-Butler City School District Board of Education*, 1990.
8. SERB 89-019, *Lakota Support Staff Assoc. v. Lakota Local School District Board of Education*, 1989.
9. SERB 89-025, *SERB v. City of Jackson*, 1989.
10. SERB 2001-002 (03-21-2001), *SERB v. Marion City School District Board of Education*, 2001.
11. Lewis and Spim, *Ohio Collective Bargaining Law*, 76.
12. *California School Employees Assn., Chapter 450 v. Tustin Unified School District* (EERB 1977).

13. Lewis and Spim, *Ohio Collective Bargaining Law*, 77.
14. Lewis and Spim, *Ohio Collective Bargaining Law*, 77.
15. Lewis and Spim, *Ohio Collective Bargaining Law*, 77.
16. SERB 89-034, *SERB v. Adena Local School District Board of Education*, 1989.
17. *NLRB v. Katz*, 369 US 736, 82 SCt 1107, 8 LEd (2d) 230 (1962).
18. Lewis and Spim, *Ohio Collective Bargaining Law*, 78.
19. *NLRB v. J. H. Bonck Co.*, 424 F(2d) 634 (5th Cir 1970).
20. *Proctor & Gamble Mfg. Co.*, 160 NLRB 334 (1966).
21. SERB 89-017, *SERB v. Montgomery County Joint Vocational School District Board of Education*, 1989.
22. SERB 89-024, *SERB v. Clermont County Sheriff*, 1989.
23. SERB 89-026, *Ohio Health Care Employees Union Dist. 1199 v. State of Ohio, Office of Collective Bargaining*, 1989.
24. SERB 89-033, *SERB v. Mayfield City School District Board of Education*, 1989.
25. SERB 89-011, *SERB v. Mentor Exempted Village Board of Education*, 1989.
26. SERB 90-017, *SERB v. Cuyahoga County Sheriffs Dept.*, 1990.
27. SERB 90-021, *SERB v. Groveport-Madison Local District Board of Education*, 1990.
28. *Service Employees International Union, Local 285* (MLRC 1976), Case No. SUPL-2006.
29. *NLRB v. Allis-Chalmers Mfg. Co.*, 388 US 175, 87 SCt 2001, 18 LEd (2d) 1123 (1967).
30. *NLRB v. Granite State Joint Bd., Textile Workers Local 1029*, 409 US 213, 93 SCt 385, 34 LEd (2d) 422 (1972).
31. *Teamsters Local 1040*, 174 NLRB 1153 (1969).
32. *NLRB v. Retail Clerks International Assn.* 203 F(2d) 165 (9th Cir 1953).
33. *Teamsters Local 70*, 183 NLRB 1330 (1970).
34. *Vaca v. Sipes*, 386 US 171, 87 SCt 903, 17 LEd(2d) 842 (1967).
35. SERB 90-006, *City of Canton v. Canton Police Patrolman's Assn.*, 1990.
36. SERB Annual Report 2001 (Columbus: Ohio State Employment Relations Board, 2001).

4

ROLES IN NEGOTIATIONS

This chapter examines the possible roles of different people in the negotiations process, including board members, the superintendent, the professional negotiator, the board attorney, and other administrators in the district.

GUIDELINES FOR THE BOARD TEAM

Every time a board of education begins to negotiate again, it has to decide who will represent the board at the bargaining table. Before looking at specific individuals who may serve in this role, it may be helpful to look at five guidelines and warnings for the board team.

1. Keep the team small. Most authorities suggest that the board team be fairly small. Having no more than five on the team makes it much easier to make decisions. During negotiations, both "sides" of the table will want to caucus, or meet privately, to discuss the proposals that they have received from the other side, consider their own positions, and then try to reach a consensus on a proposal to take back to the negotiating table. It makes sense that the larger the number of participants in the group, the more time this will take and the more difficult it will be to formulate a response.

Sometimes the teachers' negotiating groups are fairly large because they want to be sure they represent all constituent groups: elementary teachers, middle/junior high teachers, high school teachers, coaches, and other groups. In addition, the teacher association may have a structure that requires their negotiations team to meet frequently with a "house of representatives." As a result, teacher teams often have the disadvantage that they take a long time making decisions. Most boards, by contrast, have only five to seven members. Thus, a team of two to four people (not necessarily board members) should be able to represent them at the bargaining table.

2. Communicate with the schools. The board team should realize that it has to represent the board and all of the schools in the district. In even a medium-size school district, it would not be feasible for the team to have representatives from each building in the district. As a result, the team must meet with the senior administrators in each building to discuss the issues that may be raised (by either side) during negotiations. The individual school principals can be helpful to the team by telling the team the issues, grievances, and complaints heard at their schools and what changes in the contract would be helpful to them as principals.

3. Schedule experts when needed. Some board teams insist on having the business manager, curriculum leader, or personnel director present at every negotiations session, "just in case" an issue is raised that they would have to answer. This takes a great deal of the time of these experts, who mostly wait for the moment when their expertise is needed. It is better to schedule these people for specific negotiations sessions when they will be needed instead of making them part of the permanent board team.

If the teachers make a proposal about which the board team feels it needs expert advice (e.g., concerns about the middle school that only the principal can discuss adequately or questions about the health insurance plan that only the business manager can answer), then the board team should suggest that this item be put on the agenda for the next session so their expert will be available for the discussion. Usually, the teachers will appreciate the board's desire to have the right person available. In addition, this gives the board team time to prepare an adequate response, with the help of the expert.

4. The board decides who is on the board team. Sometimes the teachers will urge the board to select certain people for the board team or tell the board how many negotiators to have on the team. Or they may tell the board not to hire a professional negotiator or to include some (or all) board members on the team. Remember that the teacher union is not making these suggestions to help the board; they are trying to make negotiations better for themselves. The board, with the advice of the superintendent, should decide who represents it.

5. Teachers try to cause conflict. It is in the best interests of the teacher negotiators if there is a conflict between different board negotiators or between the negotiator(s) and the board itself. Divide and conquer. If the teachers can find ways to put individual pressure on those negotiating, they will do it. Unfortunately, these tactics even apply to using the negotiator's children (and, in a case this author observed, their grandchildren). This author recalls examples such as teachers making comments in their classes about a student's father who is on the board team, grading examinations unfairly, or denying membership in the Honor Society. Members of the board's negotiating team need to realize that these events sometimes occur and that they need to be prepared for them.

The purpose of this pressure is to cause negotiators to "ease off" or to pit one team member against another. The board team (and the board itself) needs to show a united front, and not let the other side drive a wedge between team members and exploit differences that the teachers perceive.

To remain united, board team members have to remember that they must act as a team and not negotiate, or even discuss issues, as individuals away from the table. Here is another personal experience: During a break in negotiations, a teacher negotiator approached two board negotiators at the water fountain in the school's hallway and informally discussed a couple of issues, appealing to their egos. The two board negotiators came back to the team and mentioned that they had come to an agreement on one issue. This accomplished two things for the teachers: (1) the teachers now knew that the board team was split on this issue and (2) the board team became divided philosophically—one group felt this incident was very destructive to the team's effort, while the other part of the team felt this was very helpful to getting an agreement.

Should Board Members Themselves Negotiate?

In deciding who will represent the board at the negotiations table, the board first has to decide whether or not it wants its own members to participate directly in negotiations. The teacher group, if asked, would normally recommend that board members themselves negotiate. It may be helpful to examine some of the reasons for this recommendation.

1. Board members are amateurs. Of course, there are exceptions. But, generally, board members do not have training in negotiations. The teachers would love to put up their well-trained negotiators, selected from all the teachers on the staff, backed up by active state associations, against a few board members who possibly attended a one-day state school board workshop. Who could blame them?

2. Board negotiators are "Yes" votes. When the negotiations are finally completed, the same board members who actively negotiated and came to a tentative settlement must now, by law, vote on whether to accept the settlement as a legal contract. The teachers assume that all board members on the negotiating team will automatically cast an affirmative vote at ratification time. After all, they took part in the settlement. Here is a personal experience: George was a board member who was on the negotiating team. When the tentative agreement came to the full board for ratification, George and another board member voted against it. George later told the board members (in executive session) that he had hoped that the contract would be passed, but that he felt that his constituency was against the salary part of the contract and, therefore, he should vote against it. Needless to say, the teachers were very upset because he had been at the negotiating table but voted "No." (George's constituents agreed with him, apparently, as he was reelected to the board.)

3. Board negotiators may divide the board. At times, the board may become divided when some board members negotiate and some do not. The nonnegotiating board members may think that the negotiating members have a better feel for what is going on in negotiations, have more up-to-date knowledge about negotiations, and have more control over the entire process. Some have gained power and position; some have not. This psychological problem can cause dissension on the board on actual issues on which there was not division before. It can result in mistrust and, possibly, a negative attitude toward (and vote on) anything coming from the negotiating board members.

4. Board negotiators may want to avoid conflict. While conflicts and pressure are expected at the negotiations table, it is different for board members. Board members are usually elected, sometimes with the endorsement of the teachers. They, unlike any other negotiators, have to negotiate with people who will vote and will urge others regarding how to vote in subsequent board elections. They are subject to phone calls, letters, and visits from voters who live next door or down the block. And, unlike trained negotiators, board members may be bothered more by the adversarial relationship that is often present at some negotiation sessions.

5. Board members are not administrators. Some contend that the negotiations process is an administrative function and should be delegated from the board to administrators. As emphasized in the first reason listed, the teachers would prefer amateur administrators, not trained ones.

6. It is not fair, part I. Because of the very nature of the process, the board team is very often on the defensive. Although the board may offer its own proposals, most proposals come from the teachers to the board. It may not be fair for board members, who are not trained negotiators, to have to be on the defensive.

7. It is not fair, part II. Theoretically, the teachers could negotiate with the full board (and they do so in a few cases). However, it is unrealistic, because of the numbers, for the board to negotiate with *all* the teachers. In practice, perhaps $1/2$ percent to 1 percent of the teachers negotiate, while 40 percent of the board may be involved.

Who Does the Board Select to Negotiate?

Most boards select one of the following to represent them in negotiations: the full board or one or more board members, the superintendent of schools, a professional negotiator or school attorney, an administrator (other than the superintendent), or a combination of these people.

This section examines the advantages and disadvantages of these possible negotiators for the board. Table 4.1 presents a summary of these advantages and disadvantages.

The Board The disadvantages of having board members negotiate was explored in the previous section. But are there any advantages? Surprisingly, there are some good reasons why board members should negotiate. First of all, when a board member reports back to the board on the progress of negotiations, the other board members see "one of their own" talking to them, not an administrator or outside person. This is a person with whom they have spent many hours making crucial decisions and whom they selected to become involved in negotiations because they have confidence in this person. By having a board member at the table, the board can say it hears teacher demands and feels teacher emotions directly. Some contend that it seems to increase the credibility of the board team.

In addition to the disadvantages already stated, it should be pointed out that the negotiations process is very time-consuming, and that board members (especially those who work full time) may find it difficult to schedule negotiations sessions. Finally, although having a board member on the board team may increase the credibility of the team, it may also weaken other team members in the eyes of the teacher team.

The Superintendent   Some people have very strong negative opinions about this: Because the superintendent must work with the teachers in all phases of the school, he or she should not destroy the relationship with the teachers by becoming involved in negotiations. However, others say that, if the negotiations process is an important administrative function, the superintendent must be involved. They further contend that he or she cannot ignore this responsibility anymore than responsibilities regarding the budget, personnel, or facilities of the district. In the author's opinion, the appropriateness of the superintendent's active involvement in negotiations varies from district to district and from year to year within the same district. Assuming the superintendent has the expertise and experience to negotiate (which is not always the case), there are times when the superintendent is the only person who has the confidence of both the faculty and the board. However, there are times when the superintendent's participation will damage his or her ability to deal with the faculty on other important projects that he or she may be leading personally. In the final analysis, the board and superintendent need to discuss this issue and decide whether this is the year they need the specific leadership of the superintendent in negotiations.

The Professional Negotiator/School Attorney   The professional negotiator and the school attorney have one thing in common that the teachers always point out: they cost money. Although all the other possible negotiators must take time from their regular jobs to serve on the negotiations team, the board does not have to budget extra money for their service. They do need to do this for an outside negotiator.

On the plus side, the professional negotiator makes a living by bargaining contracts. These negotiators must be good at negotiating or else they will go out of business quickly. The board who hires the experienced professional gets not only someone who is an expert at negotiations, but also someone who is negotiating at other schools, hearing similar proposals from teacher groups, and seeing which of his or her responses seems to be most acceptable. This concurrent experience at other schools is very important, especially since state teacher associations often suggest boilerplate proposals to local teachers to present at the table. While the local negotiator might find such a proposal confusing in light of local conditions, the professional negotiator will be familiar with the proposal and with proper responses.

Besides giving valuable help with contract language, this negotiator can also provide the board with accurate, current information on the dollar costs of salary and fringe-benefit settlements in other districts. Finally, the successful professional negotiator has probably developed a decent working relationship with the state association negotiators who often assist local teacher groups with negotiations.

The school attorney can have all the advantages just mentioned for the professional negotiator if the attorney spends most of his or her time negotiating. Obviously, there are many outstanding school attorneys who, while providing valuable legal advice, simply do not negotiate much at all. If such a person negotiates for only one district, the attorney cannot have the experience of the professional negotiator.

However, if the school attorney does negotiate widely, the board has another bonus. Once the contract is settled, the attorney is still in the picture, available to be called on for contract interpretation, for the wording on grievance responses, for help with grievance arbitration, and for other matters pertaining to the contract.

This extension of services of the school attorney provides a contrast to one of the objections about the professional negotiator: that the negotiator comes in to settle a contract and then disappears until the contract is due to be negotiated again.

While both board members and teachers sometimes object to outside negotiators because they can "negotiate and run" and do not have to "live with the contract," there are positive aspects of this, too. The board may sometimes find an advantage in having a negotiator who is objective, uninvolved in the local problems, not the subject of any grievances, and can support the board's stance strongly without worrying about repercussions in other areas of his or her job later in the year. Thus, the outside negotiator's leaving after the bargaining is over is both an advantage and a disadvantage.

Other Administrators   One option the board sometimes chooses is to appoint an administrator other than the superintendent to be the negotiator. This person is usually a central-office administrator, often someone in charge of personnel or business.

This individual often brings some of the advantages of the superintendent without the disadvantages. This administrator knows the district, its people, its problems, its financial situation, and its bargaining and grievance history. Communication with the superintendent and principals is easy. And if this administrator negotiates on a regular basis, he or she can develop expertise in the process and be available all year to interpret the contract. Unlike the superintendent, the central-office administrator who negotiates is less likely to suffer the negative fallout from the process since he or she is less visible in the organization than the superintendent.

The disadvantages include the fact that the negotiations process takes a great deal of the administrator's time, that he or she may not have extensive experience in negotiations, and that, while not in the same position as the superintendent, the administrator may still suffer a backlash as a result of representing the board in negotiations. This is especially true when the teachers attack the negotiator (or "kill the messenger") and try to discredit him or her for taking the strong position the board insisted be taken at the table.

Combination of People   The term "board team" has been mentioned several times in this chapter. This implies that the board decided to appoint several people to represent them at the negotiations table instead of nominating or hiring only one person to negotiate. Yet, just as boards vary across the country, so do the ways they decide to negotiate. Some do select one individual—a board member, a superintendent or central-office administrator, or a professional negotiator or school attorney. Many more, however, choose to have a group of people represent them in negotiations. (See table 4.2 for specific percentages.)

The board team is usually composed of some combination of the people mentioned previously. Sometimes building administrators (principals and assistant principals) join the team as well.

The team has the advantage of the pooled knowledge and experience of its members and is able to communicate back to the board and other administrators easily. And, if small, the team can caucus and make decisions during negotiations without taking a long time.

One important thing to remember: this team must have a leader, a **chief negotiator** who has the expertise and experience to use the knowledge that the other members can contribute. The chief negotiator is almost always one of the people named previously as possible negotiators.

The Role of the Chief Negotiator

The chief negotiator is the person at the table who speaks for the team. Some people in this capacity insist that no one else on the team ever say a word at the negotiation table; others caution their team members not to make any proposals or comments except to clarify or answer questions.

Table 4.1. Advantages and Disadvantages of People in Different Positions as Board Negotiators

	Advantages	Disadvantages
Board Member(s)	One of "their own" Board hears teachers directly Increases credibility	May be amateur Considered automatic "Yes" vote Subject to public pressure Doing an administrative function Participation is time-consuming, hard to schedule May weaken other team members
Superintendent	Too important a function to avoid The position can help during negotiations Knows the district	May hurt relations with teachers Takes time away from job
Professional Negotiator	Special expertise Extensive experience Leaves after negotiations are over	Costs money Leaves after negotiations are over
School Attorney	May have expertise May have experience Available for follow-up	Costs money
Other Administrator	Knows the district May have expertise May have experience	Takes time away from job May be some backlash

(This author can recall one chief negotiator from the state teacher association who required all the local teachers on the team to pass him written notes during sessions. No one was allowed to utter a single word.) Each chief negotiator has to assess the team and decide to what extent the members understand when it is appropriate to say something and when it is not. Regardless of the working (talking) relationship, it is the chief negotiator who presents all proposals, discusses all proposals, and responds to all proposals at the table. When the team meets together privately, each member will get a chance to contribute ideas and make comments that can help the team arrive at suitable responses and proposals.

Later, when proposals are accepted and the contract is settled, it is the chief negotiator who signs off on the proposals (described in a later chapter) and checks all language in the contract.

RESEARCH ON NEGOTIATIONS

In 1989, this author, with the help of the American Association of School Administrators, conducted a national study of school superintendents on the subject of collective bargaining, especially on the role of the superintendent and school board. In 1999, the same survey used in the 1989 study was sent again to the same school districts. This section details some of the findings of that study.[1] (Keep in mind that all responses came from school superintendents. Not all percentage totals listed will equal 100 percent, as some superintendents chose not to respond to some questions.)

1. Board composition. From a list of various categories of people who may negotiate for the board (the same categories discussed in this chapter), the superintendents were asked to identify the *one* category that reflected the person(s) who negotiated for their board. W. E. Caldwell[2] asked this same question in a 1970 survey, so his results are given in table 4.2, along with the 1989 and 1999 survey results.

Comment: The vast majority of the country's boards use a team approach to negotiations and do not use only one person or only board members. Looking at the data over the past three decades, little change can be seen in the use of a professional negotiator or attorney as the sole negotiator, al-

Table 4.2. Board Team Composition (% of all boards)

Category	1970	1989	1999
Board attorney (only)	3.0	2.0	3.5
Hired negotiator; not board attorney (only)	5.0	4.0	3.5
Superintendent (only)	1.0	6.1	5.0
Other administrators (only)	1.0	10.6	12.1
Committee of some board members (only)	45.0	11.1	13.5
The entire school board (only)	9.0	0.5	0.7
Combination of the above	37.0	65.7	59.6

though there has been an increase in the use of administrators and in the team approach, along with a decrease in cases in which board members negotiate by themselves.

2. Chief spokesperson. Who is the chief spokesperson (chief negotiator) for the board team at the table (table 4.3)?

Comment: If these figures are representative, there seems to be a change from using a board member or a professional negotiator as the chief spokesperson to using the superintendent.

3. Should the superintendent be on the board? The superintendents were asked (table 4.4): Regardless of whether or not they were on the board team, did they think they *should be* a member on this team?

Comment: While the 1989 results were not conclusive, the results in 1999 seem to favor the superintendent being a part of the negotiating team.

4. Who the superintendent would prefer to serve with him or her. The next two questions were interesting. The first asked: If the board insisted that you, as superintendent, be the chief negotiator at the table and

Table 4.3. Chief Spokesperson (% of all boards)

	1989	1999
A board member	27.6	20.6
The superintendent	17.9	22.0
A central-office administrator	17.3	16.3
A professional negotiator	21.9	16.3
The school attorney	15.3	15.6
A principal	0.0	0.0

Table 4.4.   Should the Superintendent Be on the
Board Team? (% of responses)

	1989	1999
Yes, they should be on the team	47.5	55.3
No, they should not be on the team	40.5	36.2
No opinion, or it could change yearly	11.6	8.5

you could select one (and only one) other person to serve with you, who would you *most* want to select (table 4.5)?

The second asked: Who would you *least* like to serve with you at the table (table 4.6)?

Comment: How could "board member" be at or near the top of both the most- *and* the least-desired lists? Perhaps superintendents are thinking about particular board members, who, in some cases, may be excellent and, in others, may not. Note the choice of "principal." It could be that the superintendents do not want them to be directly involved in negotiations since the process might hurt their relationships with their teachers. Board members and central-office administrators are further removed from the building-level faculty and are less likely to have the type of relationships with teachers that principals have.

5. Superintendent's role. The 1989 and 1999 superintendents were asked to respond to another of Caldwell's questions to see what changes had occurred since that study. Superintendents were asked to pick the *one* role (or the most dominant role) that they had had in negotiations (table 4.7).

Comment: More superintendents are nonparticipants today than a decade ago. Perhaps they have learned that participation is hazardous to job security and now delegate this responsibility. It makes sense that fewer su-

Table 4.5.   Who Would the Superintendent Most
Want to Serve on the Board with Him or Her
(% of responses)

	1989	1999
Board member	30.9	27.0
Central-office administrator	22.7	27.7
School attorney	22.7	18.4
Professional negotiator	17.5	18.4
Principal	5.7	5.7
Other administrator	0.5	0.0

Table 4.6. Who Would the Superintendent Least Want to Serve on the Board with Him or Her (% of responses)

	1989	1999
Board member	39.0	29.1
Principal	27.0	26.2
School attorney	9.4	15.6
Professional negotiator	8.8	9.9
Central-office administrator	8.8	4.3
Other administrator	3.8	5.0

perintendents would advise the teachers' organization along with the board. The number of superintendents who have been given "full authority" to negotiate has increased greatly since the 1970 study. This may be because the negotiations process has become more complicated and time-consuming.

6. The superintendents were asked to respond to some possible advantages and disadvantages of having board members serve on the negotiating team. Here are some of the responses:

Advantages

They agreed or strongly agreed that having board members negotiate allows them to hear teacher demands and feelings directly (73.7 percent in 1999; 85.4 percent in 1989).

It provides direct communication to other board members (73.1 percent in 1999; 76.3 percent in 1989).

It increases the credibility of the team to have board members present (62.4 percent in 1999; 69.2 percent in 1989).

Table 4.7. The Superintendent's Role or Dominant Role (% of responses)

	1970	1989	1999
Nonparticipant in negotiations	0.4	5.6	4.3
Adviser to teachers' organization only	0.0	0.0	0.0
Adviser to both teachers' organization and to the board of education	43.4	16.6	16.3
Adviser to the board only	19.1	46.0	37.6
Negotiator for the board with limited authority	31.5	15.1	19.1
Negotiator for the board with full authority	5.6	16.7	21.3

Comment: Overall, the percentages in 1999 were less than those in 1989, perhaps reflecting superintendents' opinions that there are fewer advantages to having board members on the team than there have been in the past.

Disadvantages
Board members may lack expertise (71.6 percent in 1999; 83.9 percent in 1989).

It is very time-consuming and may be hard to schedule board members (63.1 percent in 1999; 67.2 percent in 1989).

It could hurt the board member's relationship with the teachers (50.4 percent in 1999; 61.1 percent in 1989).

It causes a board member to engage in an administrative function (48.3 percent in 1999; 51.5 percent in 1989).

Comment: Because of the decreased percentages for 1999 on the "advantages" question, it might be assumed that there would be an increase in 1999 for the "disadvantages." This was not the case.

SUMMARY

This chapter began with some general guidelines for the board team and then discussed whether board members should be a part of the negotiation process. This was followed by a discussion of the advantages and disadvantages of having different people do the negotiations: the board, the superintendent, the professional negotiator or school attorney, other school administrators, or a combination of these groups. The role of the chief negotiator was explained. The chapter concluded by giving research data on the role of negotiators as perceived by the nation's superintendents. The next chapter examines the process and strategies of negotiations.

DISCUSSION QUESTIONS

1. Why is it wise for the board to have a small team? Why do the teachers often have larger teams?

2. Why is it important for the board team to "act as a team"?
3. Discuss the advantages and disadvantages of having each of the following negotiate for the board: board members themselves, the superintendent, a professional negotiator, the school attorney, other administrators.
4. Discuss the role of the chief negotiator.
5. According to the research data given, what would the typical board team look like?
6. What were some of the major differences between the 1970 and 1989/1999 research findings?
7. What could be the reason that superintendents in the study did not want principals on the negotiating team?

NOTES

1. William L. Sharp, "The Role of the Superintendent and School Board in Collective Bargaining: 1989–1999" (paper presented at the annual meeting of the Mid-Western Educational Research Association, Chicago, October 14, 1999), 10–18.

2. W. E. Caldwell, "The Superintendent's Negotiation Role," *Journal of Educational Research 64*, no. 2 (1970): 73–77.

5

NEGOTIATIONS: PROCESS AND STRATEGIES

This chapter discusses guidelines for preparing for negotiations, receiving demands from the teachers, and responding to those demands. It will conclude with specific strategies that should be helpful to those who are negotiating.

PREPARING FOR NEGOTIATIONS

Negotiating is an art—and a critical factor in employer–employee relations. Previous chapters discussed the variety of roles people play in negotiations and the typical bargaining rules and regulations that are mandated by many states.

Negotiations involve talking and listening, giving in and receiving back, and knowing when to push and when to pull back. Even the placement of personnel at the bargaining table seems to define the act of negotiations, for the team representing the school board sits on one side and a team representing the teachers sits on the other. In addition, people who spend their lives negotiating—professional negotiators—often sit on both sides of the table, lending further evidence that this process must be an important one.

Specific guidelines must be followed in preparation for the negotiations sessions; these include:

1. The board's negotiating team should be reminded that it is not their role to set board policy. That is the role of the full board. Sometimes this negotiating team includes board members who may be tempted to act as the full board and set policy. This cannot occur. The team's role is to hear teacher demands, take demands back to the board, propose alternative responses to the board, get the board's parameters for each issue, and formulate responses to take back to the table.

2. The board should demonstrate confidence in its negotiating team by giving it some leeway in making responses. If the team merely echoes the board responses and cannot make any decisions (within the board parameters), it serves as a secretary rather than as a negotiator. Thus, as mentioned previously, the board should study each issue, hear the advice of the superintendent and the board's negotiating team, and give the team its parameters for the issues. The board should be especially careful to give leeway in the area of "language" issues— those demands that do not directly involve salary and fringe benefits. The board should listen carefully to the school administrators' perspectives on these issues and learn how these teacher proposals will affect the governance of the school. On money issues such as salary, some boards will give the team a base salary figure, some will give a percentage increase, and others will give a "pool" of money for the team to work with in any way they deem appropriate.

3. Board members and administrators need to be reminded that they cannot discuss issues and possible responses with the teachers—any teachers. If the superintendent (or other administrator) feels awkward about discussing this with the board, he or she should discuss this with the board president, who can communicate this important rule to the full board. The board member who regularly meets with several teachers for pizza can undermine the entire negotiations process (from the board's point of view) if this rule is broken. A board member does not have to be specific to cause trouble; simply conveying the impression that the board is about to "give in a little bit" on an issue might be enough to damage negotiations. Some union members are adept at identifying board members who can be complimented, treated as individuals with important information and authority, and manipulated to reveal board positions without even knowing it. Everyone involved in negotiations must be cautioned about these types of manipulative situations and conversations.

4. The board (and its team) should not tell the teachers whom to select for their negotiating team any more than the teachers should tell the board whom to choose. While this may seem obvious, this rule is often broken. A board member or administrator may tell some teachers, "I hope you don't have John on the team again. Remember how he reacted last time?" or "Your UniServ director really hurt you last time. He doesn't know the school system. You really should negotiate without him." Similarly, teachers may tell the board that they want only "two negotiators" for the board team, or they may issue a directive to "Keep that attorney away from the table this year." Both the board and the teacher union should make up their own minds about who represents them.

5. Keep the board informed at all times. There should be no major surprises for the board. Many states allow the board to discuss collective bargaining strategies in executive session. If this is not permitted, the team should discuss, with the board president, the means to best inform the board throughout the negotiations process. The board does not have to be told every single proposal that went back and forth across the table. If this occurs, the board might as well go to the sessions themselves. They need to be told enough to make intelligent decisions and to get a feeling of the overall progress on the issues. Eventually, the full board will have to vote on (ratify) the document that the team negotiated. No team wants to reach this point and have some board members say they were surprised at the response the team made on an important issue.

6. The chief negotiator for the board's team should tell the board if their position on an issue is unrealistic. This writer was once told by the board to make this initial response to the teachers' first salary demand: "Offer them a 10 percent salary cut." This was unrealistic. (In this case, although the board was told that this response would not be advisable, the board insisted that this response be given. As a result, the teachers became very upset and responded by raising their salary demand—an appropriate response under the circumstances. After this waste of time, the board made a realistic response, as did the teachers. But a lot of time was wasted and the board's response created a poor beginning atmosphere.)

7. The board's team should gather the information it needs. This includes obtaining salary schedules from neighboring districts, especially those that are considered rivals and those that are similar in size, community, and financial condition. Most superintendents exchange actual master contracts (the document that contains everything resulting from the negotiation sessions) after negotiations are completed. These documents can be helpful in providing information about how other districts word certain sections that may be discussed at your sessions. In discussions with other districts who are also negotiating (or who have just concluded negotiations), determine what issues are occurring, especially ones that are new or unique. Very often, the state teachers' organization asks all (or selected) districts to pursue particular issues, and they even give the teachers the exact wording to propose in all districts (these are called "boilerplate" proposals).

To prepare for salary negotiations, the team needs to calculate the cost of the district's present schedule and the cost of other possible schedules that might be negotiated. This writer used to put the present salary schedule on a computer spreadsheet so that a new salary schedule could be created by just entering a new beginning salary amount. Of course, the original schedule was designed so that all salaries in the schedules (or "cells") were calculated from one base salary. Many districts have such a schedule. In addition, a scattergram was made showing the location of every teacher on the schedule. When the schedule is multiplied by the number of teachers at each step, the cost of the schedule is determined. (Of course, this does not include the many additions that may be given, such as longevity pay.) Prior to the first session, it is useful to insert various possible base salaries and print out the new potential salary schedules and the resulting cost of each schedule.

8. The administrators in the district should look at the present contract language and recall problems that occurred as a result of specific sections. They should submit suggested changes to the superintendent for consideration. The negotiating team should discuss these suggested changes and take the best ones to the board for further discussion. Some school districts find it helpful to discuss specific proposals with the school attorney, a professional negotiator, or the state school boards' association or superintendents' association.

The board should consider making its own proposals for several reasons:

1. Some proposals are written to correct sections in the current contract. These usually originate from the suggestions made by the school administrators. In considering such proposals, the team should be able to refer to specific problems posed by these current sections of the contract. The board will not get far in negotiating by simply stating, "We don't like this section."

2. Some proposals are new for the contract. The team needs to be able to justify why each of these is necessary.

3. Some new proposals presented at the table as serious proposals are really "give-away" items. These items are plausible and important proposals that would be helpful if accepted—but the team does not expect them to be included in the final contract. These are useful in that they can be "dropped" from consideration by the board's team and paired with items the teachers are dropping. This writer once proposed that all teachers who received an unsatisfactory yearly evaluation be "held on step" (not moved to the next salary step the following year). Needless to say, this was not very popular and received strong opposition from the teachers' team. The value of this item was shown near the end of negotiations, when the board's team finally dropped this proposal. The teachers were so glad to get rid of this proposal that all other items were settled that night and the contract was agreed upon. It is interesting to note that the same proposal was made the next time the teams negotiated and was accepted by the teachers. Apparently, the teachers decided that the board really wanted this proposal and would stick with it this time.

4. Finally, it is useful to have some board proposals on the table in the event that the state provides for fact-finding or arbitration when an impasse occurs (negotiations are not progressing; neither side will accept any of the other's proposals). If an arbitrator has to make a decision or recommendation regarding the final contractual agreement, he often likes to give something to both sides, accepting certain items from the teachers and certain items from the board's

team. If the board has no proposals, the arbitrator cannot choose a board proposal.

RECEIVING DEMANDS IN NEGOTIATIONS

The teachers are usually prepared to present their proposals (demands) at the first bargaining session. The board's team should be in a "receiving" mode: listening carefully to each proposal, taking notes if it helps, and asking questions to clarify the proposals. Do not make any responses to these early proposals—simply listen and clarify. Ask the union to explain each proposal in terms of the local conditions and problems since some of these proposals may be "boilerplate." If they cannot give good, specific examples explaining why the item is necessary in the district, their position is much weaker on that item. And keep that in mind for the future sessions.

Do not overreact or ridicule any of the proposals. What may seem silly, unnecessary, or insulting to the board's team may seem perfectly sane to the teachers' representatives. There will be ample time later to react appropriately.

After the board's team has listened to all the proposals (the teachers may ask to present some others later) and asked appropriate questions, the board representatives should thank them and state that they will meet and formulate responses and proposals to give to them at the next session. Do not state (or agree) that the board will respond to every single proposal the next time.

The team should meet with the full board in closed session (where legal) to discuss the teacher proposals. Hopefully, the board will not require that all members be given written and oral explanations of each proposal. As stated earlier, they might as well attend the sessions if they do this. The board should hear the proposals and discuss them in the context of the original parameters they established. These guidelines may have to be altered, but probably not at this time. The board should not establish an unalterable position (e.g., board's final salary offer). Neither the board nor the teachers know what the final agreements will be; both sides have to be somewhat flexible at this point. There comes a time when the board has to take a strong stand and say, "This is it." But this does not happen at this first meeting.

RESPONDING TO THE DEMANDS

Often, the board will receive many teacher proposals. Ascertain which ones are really important to them and why. Ask questions in order to have them justify each proposal in terms of local school conditions. This will eliminate some of the proposals.

Because many of the proposals will not be acceptable at all to the board, at least in their original condition, the board's team may be tempted to readily accept a proposal when one is discovered that is fully acceptable to the team. However, the board should not automatically accept any proposal, but try to get something in exchange for their acceptance. This process takes time and usually does not occur very early in the negotiations. One strategy to avoid either accepting or rejecting a proposal currently under discussion is to state, "I think we may be able to work something out on this concept eventually." This tells the union that the board is not rejecting a specific proposal but may simply need to modify it somewhat before it is acceptable.

Also, the teacher team may present a proposal that is unacceptable as written but that deals with a concern recognized as legitimate. Rejecting this proposal might cause problems since the teachers feel it is very important. The board should tell the teacher representatives that it recognizes the problem, that problem is legitimate, and that the board understands their concern. While their present proposal is not something that can be accepted as written, the board "will try to work something out" and get back to them in order to resolve the problem in some way.

While this writer does not like to reject teacher proposals early in the process (and create a negative atmosphere almost before anything has started), the board's team should not give the impression that an unacceptable proposal is acceptable. Thus, the board's team can state, "I see a lot of problems with this one" or "I would have a hard time selling this one to the board." Later, the board can come back and say that studying this proposal showed that the original opinion was correct: the proposal is not acceptable.

The board should not feel that it has to answer every single teacher proposal at the first meeting in which it presents responses. This writer made that mistake the first time he negotiated. After receiving all the teachers' proposals and deciding that nearly all of them should be rejected, at least initially, he presented the teachers with a written list of responses consisting mostly of the following:

Item 4: No
Item 5: No
Item 7: No
Item 8: No

Needless to say, this did not contribute to a positive start. It would have been better to have proceeded as outlined previously.

Finally, the board's team should see if some minor teacher proposals are acceptable or could be accepted if paired with some of the board's minor proposals. This technique demonstrates the willingness to bargain and also provides evidence of that fact in the event that an unfair labor practice (failure to bargain in good faith, as discussed in chapter 3) is filed against the board.

BARGAINING STRATEGIES

Once the administration has received the demands of the teachers and has started to respond to them, it is important to note when to respond and how to respond to the teachers. Here are some suggestions and strategies for these negotiations sessions.

1. The board should not refer to any teacher proposals not recently mentioned. After several sessions of negotiating, the board's team may notice that the teachers have not mentioned a particular proposal for several sessions. Although curious about this, the board should not refer to the teachers' missing proposal. The board should leave it to them to bring it up. It is possible that the union has decided to drop the proposal. Perhaps they realized that it would not be accepted; perhaps they were embarrassed that they could not defend it adequately and did not want to bring it up again. If the board mentions it, the teachers might feel they have to support it again. The board should hope instead that the proposal has died a quiet death. If the teachers do bring it up, nothing has been lost. The board can remark that it assumed that the proposal had been dropped, and that some of the concessions the board had made were based on that assumption. This may help the board get additional concessions.

2. The board should not start a session by agreeing to one of the union's proposals from the last meeting: the teachers may have altered the proposal to make it more acceptable or may have dropped it entirely. The teachers will be delighted if the board accepts a proposal that they have decided to drop.

It should be mentioned that a bargaining session often concludes with both sides agreeing on which items will be discussed the next time. If the board has agreed to come back to the table with a response to class-size proposal number twelve, then it should do it. But the board should not agree to other proposals from the past until the teachers' present position on those issues has been determined.

3. If possible, the board should try to structure "proposal acceptance" so that the board is finally agreeing to a rewritten proposal from the union instead of having the teachers agree to the board's restructured proposal. From a psychological standpoint, the board is saying, "Yes" and "We agree with you" or "We give in," although the board finds the proposal quite acceptable. While the board probably could have written the final acceptable language on this topic itself and the union would have agreed with it, it is better to have them submit it to the board and have the board accept their proposal. There may come a point when the board can state, "We have accepted five of your proposals during the last two sessions and you have not accepted any of ours during the same time. Let's have some concessions in our direction." It also helps the teachers' team when the board accepts their proposals: they can go back to their members and state that the board "gave in" on certain issues and accepted the teachers' wording (even though they may know better.)

4. The board's team should attempt to negotiate a "management rights" clause into the contract if there is not one in the contract already. This recognizes the rights and powers of the board and preserves board authority. It may also be helpful in the event that arbitration over grievances occurs (discussed in chapter 10). The appendix to this chapter outlines three examples of some management rights clauses that have been negotiated. (While better clauses than these can be written, these have been negotiated and placed into actual contracts.)

5. Examine the grievance section of the master contract carefully. A grievance procedure section is usually found in a master contract. In fact, some states require it in all teacher agreements. Here are some ideas when negotiating this part of the contract (and some possible proposal ideas for the board to consider for an existing grievance section).

- Make sure that the word "grievance" is carefully and narrowly defined. It should be a "violation of the contract" (some may say an "alleged" violation of the contract). The important word here is "contract." A grievance should not involve anything that is not contained explicitly in the contract. The grievance should be placed in writing, stating the contract provision that has been violated. Simply stating that the contract has been violated is insufficient. For example, the grievance should state that "Article V, Section 2a" has been violated. The grievance should also state the remedy the teacher seeks. In addition, the board should be sure that the time lines are somewhat restrictive in the amount of time allowed between the violation and the filing of the grievance, and that the time lines are somewhat liberal in making an administrative response.
- One proposal that this writer made in an old grievance section was to drop the "board step" in the grievance process. (This contract had steps at the principal level, the superintendent level, the board level, and—unfortunately—binding arbitration.) Knowing that the teachers would not agree to eliminating the arbitration step, the proposal suggested that the board step be dropped. The teachers accepted this, perhaps because they thought it would shorten the whole process. From the administrative standpoint, dropping the board step took away the possibility of a public appearance at a board meeting, which sometimes results in board members saying the wrong thing and newspapers printing news of the "violation" before an answer can be given. After the superintendent gives a response under this new grievance procedure, the teachers have to accept it or go to arbitration. Going to the board is not an option. The board is instructed that they are no longer a part of the process and

should not even listen to any discussion pertaining to any grievance issue. (Of course, the superintendent should keep the
board informed of any grievances.)

- If the grievance section contains arbitration that cannot be eliminated, the board should try to limit the authority of the arbitrator. The arbitrator should confine the rulings to the actual contract and not use personal interpretation of other documents or
the law.

**6. To repeat an important principle of negotiating, the board
should try to make the union negotiators look good to their
teachers**. Remember, they have received many demands from the
teachers that they will not be able to satisfy. The teachers have been told
that they should have a big raise and receive new rights in the new contract; moreover, their team will have to come back to them with a salary
schedule that is less than they wanted and with fewer new rights than
they desired. So, the teacher team will have to sell the new contract to
the teachers.

**7. The board should be sure to keep some noneconomic items
on the table while salary is still being discussed**. Sometimes the
teachers will suggest that all noneconomic items be negotiated before
any economic items are discussed. (Of course, most are really related to
money in some way.) They may state, "Let's get them all out of the way."
The board should not agree to this strategy. Remember, when money
items surface, there is usually only one way to go: up. With the other
items, it is possible to negotiate with the language. So, when the mone-
tary items are raised under this union strategy, the board may not have
any items to bargain with at all.

Typically, noneconomic items are the subject of talks at the very beginning of negotiations, with salary and other cost items entering soon
after the beginning. The board should be sure to keep some noneconomic items on the table so that the union has to make some concessions in exchange for the increases they will get in salary. In short, the
board should get something for its money.

8. Sometimes it helps to negotiate in "packages." This is especially useful if there are too many proposals to allow negotiators to
look at the whole picture at once, or if the end of negotiations is at

hand and there are a few important items to consider. Here is an example.

Assume that the union has a number of issues on the table:

Teacher proposals

1. XXXXX (We will not name each one)
2. XXXX
3. XXXXXXXXX
4. Class size should be no more than twenty-two. [Actually, a class-size proposal would probably be more complicated than this.]
5. XXXXXX
6. The base salary should be $32,000.
7. XXXX
8. XXXXXXXXXX
9. Insurance coverage should be increased to include dental, vision care, and prescription medicine.
10. XXXXXX
11. XXXXXXXXX

Likewise, the board also has some items still on the table. One of their items concerns the evaluation of teachers. (There are a number of good proposals in this area.)

The board team might offer a "package" proposal consisting of the following:

Board package

1. a base salary of $29,500 [Reacting to union item number 6];
2. an increase in insurance coverage to include dental [reacting to union item number 9], and
3. a change in teacher evaluation as outlined in board item number 3 [We did not list the board items, but this was the third one.]

This package consists of three and only three items. The union has three options: (1) it can accept the entire package as stated above; (2) it can reject the entire package as is, or (3) it can propose a package in return. What the union *cannot* do is accept one or two of the preceding three items only. In other words, these three items come as a package deal.

Using a package like this has the advantage of narrowing the issues to a manageable number and, from the board's standpoint, making sure that the board has an issue on the table to negotiate, too. It is a method to get both sides to make concessions—to make both sides negotiate.

9. Timing is important. Both the board and the teachers will keep an eye on legislative action and settlements in other districts. Sometimes the board may want to settle before another district settles; the union may want to see the outcome from the other district in hopes that it puts more pressure on the local board. Also, with respect to timing, the board should be careful about giving a "final" offer to the teachers. If the board gives them its "final" salary offer, for example, and later raises the amount due to a strike, concessions, time, pressure, or whatever, the board's word on future "final" offers will be suspect, to say the least. The board's team should not say "final" unless it means it and the full board is willing to back it up. (This writer once was negotiating for a board that insisted on giving the teachers a final salary offer. Each board member signed the proposal to the teachers to show their commitment to this final offer. As we walked out of the building a few minutes later, one board member said to another, "I think we should rethink our last offer." The other board member jumped all over him for saying that after he had just signed the proposal.)

When the board is offering the union a salary figure and is tempted to say it is the final one, it might state the following: "We are getting awfully close to our top" or "This is as high as the board has authorized, and we have no reason to think they will go higher." While neither of these statements is ideal, they do provide some leeway in the event that the amount is raised later. In negotiations, credibility is very important. When the board does say, "That's it," it wants to be believed.

10. Finally, when everything is settled, always let the union think they forced the board "to the wall" and that the board gave them the last available penny for teacher salaries. The board team and all board members need to be instructed to do the same. If one person tells a teacher, "You could have gotten another hundred dollars apiece if you had held out another session" or "We would have given in to you on insurance, but you gave up on it and we were happy about that," it will be remembered for a long time—at least until it is time to negotiate again.

SUMMARY

This chapter began with some guidelines for those who are preparing to negotiate. It then discussed what the board team should do when receiving demands and responding to those demands. The chapter concluded with negotiations strategies and introduced the concept of "management rights" and the idea of negotiating in "packages." The next chapter, the third on actual negotiations, will discuss some general procedures that should be helpful to the negotiator.

DISCUSSION QUESTIONS

1. What are some reasons why the board team should consider presenting some proposals of their own?
2. How should the board team react at the initial negotiations session?
3. What are "boilerplate" proposals?
4. Discuss the communications between the team and the full board.
5. Discuss the possible mistake in taking a strong stand and stating, "This is it. This is the board's final offer."
6. What is wrong with asking the teacher team about one of their proposals they have not mentioned recently?
7. What is the reason the board team tries to structure negotiations so that they accept the teachers' proposals?
8. Describe a management rights clause.
9. What are some proposals for improving the grievance section?
10. Describe how to negotiate in packages.

APPENDIX: MANAGEMENT RIGHTS

Example I

The Association recognizes that the Board of Education has full authority and responsibility under the laws of the State of _____ and responsibility to this Agreement with respect to employment, tenure, or discharge of any of its employees. The Board of Education and the Association recognize, understand, and agree that the Board cannot enter into any agreement that impairs the authority vested in the Board by law, and that the provisions of any professional negotiations agreement that is negotiated by the Board with the Association cannot conflict with the provisions of the Constitution of the United States and of the State of _____, the _____ School Code, as well as the decisions of the Courts of the United States and of the State of _____. The Association recognizes that in the operation of the schools, the Board is guided by the regulations and criteria for the approval, recognition and accrediting of schools promulgated by the State Superintendent of Schools of _____ County, the North Central Association, as well as Federal Education Agencies when applicable. The Association recognizes the Board's right to direct the operation of the schools and the Board's right to delegate to its administrators the assignment of all certified personnel, provided that such rights shall be exercised in conformity with the provisions of this Agreement.

Example 2

The Board retains and reserves unto itself all powers, rights, functions, authority, duties, and responsibilities conferred upon and vested in it by the statutes and court decisions of the State of _____, which are not specifically limited by the express language of this Agreement, provided, however, that no such right shall be exercised so as to violate any of the specific provisions of this Agreement.

Example 3

The _____ Board of Education on its own behalf and on the behalf of the electors of the district, hereby retains and reserves unto itself, without limitation, all powers, rights, authority, duties, and responsibilities conferred upon and vested in it by the laws and the Constitution of the State of _____, and of the United States including, but without limiting the generality of the foregoing, the right:

1. *To exercise executive management and administrative control over the school system and its properties and facilities.*

2. *To hire all employees subject to the provisions of the law and subject to the limitations of this Agreement.*

3. *To establish grade levels and courses of instruction, including special programs, and to provide for athletic, recreational, and social events for students, all as deemed necessary and/or advisable by the Board.*

4. *To control the means and methods of instruction, the selection of textbooks and other teaching materials, aids, and equipment.*

6

GENERAL PROCEDURES
FOR NEGOTIATIONS

While strategy (chapter 5) is important in negotiations, it is also important to establish good procedures for the team. This chapter discusses some suggestions for organizing the work, handling the media, and scheduling, as well as for other techniques to help the team.

ORGANIZATION

Negotiators can become inundated with paper if they do not have a procedure for dealing with it. At every negotiations session, each side of the table will usually present several proposals and counterproposals. Some parts of one proposal will be agreed upon by both sides while other proposals will have no agreed-upon sections. If, for example, the teachers present twenty proposals, the board responds to fifteen of them, and the teachers respond back with twelve counterproposals, a negotiator already has a lot of paper and discussion to organize.

1. Organize paperwork in a three-ring binder. One good start is to purchase a large, three-ring binder with dividers. Use a different section of the binder for each major proposal. For example, have sections reserved for proposals on salary issues, teacher evaluation, extracurricular activity pay, class size, and any other areas in which either side has

made a proposal. The back-up data, salary schedules, and possible counterproposals can be kept in an appendix in the back of the binder for
easy reference.

2. Identify each proposal. Identify each proposal by date, time, and
"side." For example, if the teachers in the Rockville Education Association (REA) submit a class-size proposal to the board team, it can be
marked "REA, 3/6" in one corner to show that it originated from the
REA team on March 6. If the teachers do not have anything labeled on
their proposal, the board's chief negotiator might state, "I have your
class-size proposal and will mark it 'REA, 3/6.'" Hopefully, the teachers
will begin to identify later proposals on their own.

When the board responds in writing, its team should also mark its
proposals (e.g., "Board, 3/6"). When two or more proposals are from the
same side on the same topic on the same day, it is helpful to put the time
down as well: "REA, 3/6, 3:14 P.M."

When all proposals are identified in this manner, it is easy to put them
in the binder in the correct order, with the latest one on top. No one
should have to ask, "Which of these evaluation proposals is their last
one?" The dates and times should give the answer.

While it may seem somewhat unnecessary to someone new to negotiations, identifying proposals in this way means it is possible to leave an issue on the table for a couple of weeks, not discuss it at all, and then return
to it without any prior notice. That is when good organization pays off.

3. Sign off on agreed-upon language. When both sides agree on
a language section, whether a single sentence or several paragraphs, the
chief negotiators of both sides should sign off (or initial) that section and
date it. Each side should be sure that it has at least one copy of the ini-
tialed and dated section for its records. This goes in the binder in the appropriate section, on top, because it is the final version of that section.

As stated in the strategy section of the last chapter, it is useful for psychological reasons to try to structure the negotiations so that the board
is agreeing to a final proposal made by the teachers. If all proposals are
identified throughout the negotiations process, the board will always
know whether they are agreeing to a teacher proposal or need to extend
the process one more step in order to accomplish this.

4. Take good notes. Someone on the board team should take good
notes during the negotiations sessions. While the chief negotiator may

be able to do this, or may have to do it because of the size and makeup of the team, it is helpful to have someone else on the team take these notes. Obviously, written proposals do not need to be copied into the notes, but it is helpful to write down which side presented which proposal and *why* they presented it. In other words, write down the major points of the arguments made in favor of each proposal. These notes are useful for several reasons:

1. They help in the overall organization of the proposals.
2. They help remind the team of the teachers' arguments so that they can better discuss them with other administrators and with the board of education.
3. If the board is accused of an unfair labor practice, such as refusing to negotiate, it can use these notes as evidence. (Evidence that may be thrown out in a court of law is often allowed at administrative hearings.)
4. The notes may be helpful when the contract is being interpreted months after an agreement has been reached. If both sides have discussed what a section *means* and this is in the notes, the notes will help in interpretation. And, if a disagreement results in arbitration, the notes can help there as well.

TIMING

In the negotiations process, timing is often important. Here are some suggestions regarding scheduling of meetings and presentation of proposals.

1. Do not rush. Sometimes the teachers will suggest establishing a schedule of meetings. It is recommended that both sides agree only on the next two times at the most. Similarly, the teachers may suggest that everyone negotiate nonstop all day (or, preferably, all night), especially if the teachers are on strike. While long sessions can sometimes be productive (if both sides are willing to negotiate and a settlement is at hand), these long sessions are often fruitless and frustrating. Proposals, caucuses, and discussions expand to fill the time available. Just as much can be accomplished in two-hour sessions.

It should be remembered that some teacher groups try to wear the board team down physically, mentally, and emotionally. It is to their advantage to negotiate against a team that has already put in a full day's work elsewhere and plans on staying up nearly all night to negotiate. As stated previously, this is especially true during a strike. The teachers have no other responsibilities, while the board team members have all their regular responsibilities and jobs as well as negotiations. Finally, having most, or all, of the board members present is an open invitation to an all-night session, under the guise of: "Let's settle this thing while the whole board is here to make decisions." A few teacher groups have been known to take a perverse delight in keeping board members up all night.

2. Meet and negotiate when there is a reason. If both sides are willing to negotiate—really negotiate—and are prepared, then both sides should do so. But if one side refuses to budge on all the issues, it is silly to sit there for hours getting madder and madder. When things come to a standstill at the table, call off the session and go home. Time may help, and pressure from outside may lead the other side to modify its position or at least become serious about beginning to negotiate. "Give and take" does not imply that the board has to do all the giving and the teachers all the taking. Each side has the right to expect the other side to negotiate in good faith.

3. Teachers will compare salaries. No teacher organization wants to look bad in relation to the other districts with which it compares itself.

So, if salary has not been settled at a nearby or rival district, the teachers may delay settling locally until they know what the settlement is going to be in the other district(s). The board team should recognize this need but also should insist that progress be made. As detailed in chapter 5, the board should not agree to postpone the salary portion of negotiations until all other proposals are decided, any more than it should agree to surrender language issues because the district cannot afford a substantial salary raise.

4. In the beginning . . . If the board knows prior to any negotiations that it will present very few proposals to the teachers, the board team should tell the teachers that fact and suggest that they curtail their number of proposals, with the board "responding in kind" to this reduction. Obviously, this has to be a suggestion, not an insistence, or it could approach being an unfair labor practice. This technique is especially practical when the two sides are meeting to "roll over" a contract for another year and do not anticipate the usual cover-to-cover (of the contract) negotiations.

5. At the end . . . Early in negotiations, when both sides are agreeing on overall procedures and schedules, the board team should insist that all proposals be presented early—in the first two to three sessions. Neither side should be allowed to surprise the other side with a proposal near the end of negotiations. This author, having witnessed such attempts, calls this the "Lieutenant Columbo" routine (as when TV's Columbo, a police detective, starts to leave the room, reaches the door, then turns around and says, "Oh, Ma'am, there's just one more thing . . ."). This is a pressure tactic, effective at the end of negotiations. Just when the board feels everything is agreed upon and the team is delighted that the process will be successfully concluded in a few minutes, the teacher team throws in "one more thing" (usually minor) in hopes that the present atmosphere will allow this point to be included in the contract. Instead, throw it back out, close the door on Columbo, and remind them of their agreement (check notes for date and time) that nothing would be proposed at the last moment.

TALKING

The individual who talks at the negotiations table as well as the individual who talks to the media (and when) are important considerations. Here are two points to remember.

1. Agree on talking at the table. As stated in chapter 4, the person selected or hired as the chief negotiator is the spokesperson for the board team at the table. This person needs to meet with the team and discuss how talking at the table should be handled: whether others are allowed to talk and under what circumstances. The purpose of a caucus should be explained as well as who is allowed to call a caucus and how the notification of the caucus is to be made to the other negotiators on the team.

2. Talking to the media. Usually, negotiations are done in private, away from the public and the press. Most of the states that have both an open meetings (sunshine) law and a collective bargaining law permit negotiations to be carried out in private. In fact, it is probably an unfair labor practice in those states to insist upon open, public negotiations.

Since the results of negotiations are important to the community and a major news story for the press, the media will ask for progress reports on the negotiations sessions. Often, both sides agree on a news blackout from the very beginning. The teachers, who often request this, have another understandable motive: they do not want the public to know the quantity and quality of their proposals. While the teachers know that many of their proposals will be dropped and that their initial salary demands are way too high, the public would not necessarily understand this.

Most of the media today understand the need for privacy in negotiations and respect it. Once a "tentative settlement" is reached, the media should be so informed and told that specifics in the settlement cannot be disclosed until the teacher representatives have had a chance to present the settlement to their members for a vote. (It is recommended that the teachers vote on ratification prior to the board vote.) Once both sides have ratified the agreement, it is suggested that representatives of both sides hold a joint press conference or issue a joint press release on the major contents of the agreement.

OTHER CONSIDERATIONS AND SUGGESTIONS

Finally, some specific contract provisions should be discussed in order to avoid infringement upon managerial prerogatives and to clarify what is in the contract.

1. Do not agree to state statutes. Sometimes teachers will propose that the board accept into the contract rights that they already possess by state statute. Their argument is that they already have the right anyway, so the board is not giving up anything by agreeing to it being in the contract. The board should recall that a teacher can file a grievance on anything in the contract that he or she feels has been violated.

For example, if the state provides for a thirty-minute, duty-free lunch period for all teachers, and the district assigns a teacher in such way that the teacher feels that he does not have thirty minutes for lunch, his only legal recourse is to file charges against the board or hope that the state takes some action. If the same provision is also contractual language, this teacher can easily file a grievance without spending much time or any money.

A personal example: A high school teacher, John, was scheduled for supervision duty from 10:30 to 11:00, with lunch from 11:00 to 11:25, and a class at 11:30. Since the thirty-minute, duty-free lunch language was in the contract, John filed a grievance. The administration shortened John's supervision assignment to 10:30 until 10:55 and lengthened his lunch to 10:55 until 11:25. John filed another grievance stating that he did not really have thirty minutes for lunch because his supervision ended at 10:55 and lunch also began at 10:55. He needed five minutes to get to the cafeteria for lunch. This despite the fact that his 10:30–10:55 supervision assignment was in *the cafeteria!* This grievance went all the way to arbitration and cost both sides several hundred dollars. By the time it was heard by the arbitrator, it was another school year and the point was moot. Avoid state statutes in the contract because they become both grievable and negotiable.

2. Consider a Memorandum of Understanding. Occasionally, both sides can agree on a concept, but the board may not want to include it in the contract because it becomes grievable and negotiable. Yet, the board wants to show good faith by having something in writing about the topic.

A way around this dilemma is to write a **Memorandum of Understanding**, a side letter, which is *not* a part of the contract. This letter, sometimes typed on district stationery like a letter, may actually be printed with the contract and included as a final page. But be sure everyone knows it is not actually contractual by putting these words on the letter: "This Memorandum of Understanding is not a part of the Contract." An example is shown is figure 6.1.

Memorandum of Understanding

(NOT A PART OF THE CONTRACT)

In order to facilitate and maintain the direction of the Board of Education on class size, a Class-Size Committee shall be established within one month of the signing of this Memorandum. The Committee will be comprised of one teacher elected from the staff of each school, two principals, the Assistant Superintendent for Instruction, and one Board member.

By January 15, the Committee shall make recommendations for changes in class size to the Superintendent for his final review and recommendations to the Board of Education. The Superintendent will make his recommendations to the Board of Education and report the recommendation of the Committee by February 15.

On the evening the Superintendent reviews all recommendations with the Board of Education, all Committee members will be invited to attend the meeting.

Negotiator for Teachers   Negotiator for Board

Date_____

Figure 6.1. Memorandum of Understanding

3. Use the sidebar. During the negotiations process, there will come a time when progress is slow. Sometimes, the two chief negotiators will meet away from the table (down the hall, on the phone, at another district where both are negotiating) and discuss the issues, trying to find an area of agreement. This is called a **sidebar**. This is probably done most often by two professional negotiators who meet in other districts to negotiate as well. Caution must be used so that other negotiators on the team do not decide to pursue this method on their own, as described in chapter 4. Only the experienced negotiator should use this means to try to get negotiations moving again. And this negotiator must have the full confidence of the team in order to engage in this practice. Needless to say, any discussions in a sidebar are unofficial. All proposals must be formally made and accepted at the table.

4. Consider a reopener. While it is the feeling of this author that, during the life of the contract, any contract article can be renegotiated if *both* sides wish to do so, sometimes both sides agree ahead of time to **reopen** the contract at a specific time for a specific purpose, and only for that purpose.

For example, both sides may agree on a two-year contract but not on the salary schedule for the second year (or on extracurricular pay or teacher evaluation). The contract can state that the term, or length, of the contract is two years (the actual dates are specified), but that this one item will be reopened for negotiations the next year, while everything else in the contract stays the same. See figure 6.2 for an example of a reopener statement.

5. Zip it up. It is suggested that the board propose a **zipper clause** for the contract. The purpose of a zipper clause is to declare, in contract language, that the contract contains all the agreed-upon issues and that neither side is obligated to negotiate anything in the contract for the duration of the agreement. See figure 6.3 for an example of a zipper clause.

SUMMARY

This chapter began with some hints on how to organize the huge amount of paper that is part of the negotiations process. This discussion included suggestions on how to mark proposals and identify those that have been

---
Term of Agreement

(*Note to readers:* the second paragraph below is the reopener statement.)

A.This contract shall be effective as of August 17, 2004, and shall continue in effect through August 16, 2006.

B. For 2005–2006, the Teachers' Association may negotiate with the Board on salary, extracurricular activity pay, and health insurance; the Board may negotiate with the Association on any one Article from this Contract.

C.This Contract is made and entered into on the 27th day of August, 2004, by and between the Board of Education of Rockville Schools, heretofore referred to as the "Board," and the Rockville Education Association, heretofore referred to as the "Association."

This Contract is so attested to by the parties whose signatures appear below:

For the Board of Education   For the Association

_____   _____

_____   _____

_____   _____

Figure 6.2.   Reopener Statement

agreed to and on the purpose of taking good notes. This was followed by some general comments on matters such as timing, when to negotiate, who should talk at the table, and how to deal with the media. The chapter then introduced the "memorandum of understanding," the "sidebar," the "reopener," and the "zipper clause," giving examples where appropriate. The

All matters within the scope of bargaining have been negotiated and agreed upon. The terms and conditions set forth in this Contract represent the full and complete understanding and commitment between the Board and the Association and supercede and cancel all previous Contracts between the parties. Both parties, for the life of this contract, voluntarily and unqualifiedly waive any right which might otherwise exist under law to negotiate any matter, and agree that the other shall not be obligated to bargain collectively with respect to any subject in this Contract or with respect to any subject not specifically referred to in this Contract, even though the subject may not have been within the knowledge or contemplation of the parties at the time they negotiated this Contract.

Figure 6.3.   Zipper Clause

next chapter is a departure from the past three chapters, which discussed procedures at the negotiating table. It will discuss the role of nonverbal communication in the negotiations process.

DISCUSSION QUESTIONS

1. Describe how a negotiator might organize the paperwork for negotiations; how the proposals from each side might be identified.
2. Name several reasons why it is useful to take notes during negotiations.
3. How can the board team avoid the "Lieutenant Columbo" routine?
4. Discuss the role of the media in negotiations.
5. Why should the board not agree to put a state statute in the contract?
6. Discuss the use of a memorandum of understanding.
7. Define "sidebar," "reopener," and "zipper clause."
8. Discuss the purpose of the union's desire to "negotiate nonstop until everything is settled."

7

NONVERBAL COMMUNICATION

Vicki Braden Sharp

During the negotiations process, utilizing and evaluating nonverbal communication may be extremely important in controlling the mood as well as the outcome of the sessions. Often, points can be made quite subtly or most dramatically using nonverbal communication. This chapter contains suggestions and examples of nonverbal communication—information to consider before and during collective bargaining.

DEFINITION OF NONVERBAL COMMUNICATION

After preparing for negotiations by reviewing the statistics and facts, a careful review of the forms and functions of nonverbal communication may be extremely beneficial. A review may serve as a reminder of the importance of nonverbal communication. In fact, continuing to develop skills in interpreting nonverbal communications should assist the negotiator in obtaining information from others involved in the process and may provide him or her a needed advantage. Being aware of the ways messages are transmitted also may help negotiators avoid inadvertently sending nonverbal signals that compromise the negotiations.

What is nonverbal communication? Quite simply, nonverbal communication is any part of the communication process that does not use words. Hickson and Stacks define it "as a process whereby people, through the intentional or unintentional manipulation of normative actions and expectations (other than words themselves) express experiences, feelings, and attitudes in order to relate to and control themselves, others, and their environments."[1]

Nonverbal communication includes not only assumptions made when observing physical appearance, body posture, and gestures, but also messages transmitted by the size, shape, color, and temperature of a room and the location of people in that room. A comparison of the environment of a decorated shopping mall during the holidays to that of a silent, simple church might be helpful in understanding the impact of nonverbal communication. Noticing the feelings associated with being in unfamiliar surroundings as opposed to being in a common location may provide clues to the way symbols are perceived in our environment.

RESEARCH ON NONVERBAL COMMUNICATION

When considering how people are manipulated and how they manipulate others, the importance of understanding and using appropriate nonverbal communication should become obvious. Some research indicates that nonverbal communications account for 60 to 70 percent of what people communicate to one another. In his book *Silent Messages*, Albert Mehrabian suggested that people communicate through media other than words much more than through the spoken word, and that approximately 93 percent of emotional messages are transmitted nonverbally. Although researchers believe that this percent is too high, they do agree that the majority of communication is nonverbal.

Advances in theoretical awareness and in the methodologies used to conduct research in nonverbal communication are expanding rapidly. Although the importance of understanding the implications of this research cannot be denied, much of what educators acknowledge regarding nonverbal communication is based solely upon experience. Unfortunately, this knowledge often is not enough when considering the influence educators exert on students, parents, peers, and the community. Furthermore, the information could be based on erroneous perceptions or interpretations. Being a good verbal and nonverbal communicator is absolutely essential to being an effective educator and successful negotiator.

Although at the university level methods and education classes provide information regarding the current research and best practices in education, courses on nonverbal communication seldom are offered or required in education departments. A review of course offerings in business departments, however, shows that courses involving negotiations and nonverbal communications there are common. Of interest may be a recent posting on the Internet announcing a three-day workshop, costing in excess of $10,000 plus travel and accommodations and focusing on nonverbal communications for the business professional.

Even though information regarding the most current research could be quite valuable for negotiators and educators, such a presentation is beyond the scope of this chapter. Although some research has become outdated before going to print, some findings of research involving nonverbal communication have been fairly consistent and may provide the negotiator with a needed advantage in the negotiations process. The information that follows should be used for a brief review prior to beginning negotiations. Because the areas most likely to affect contract negotiations are physical environment, personal attributes, and body language, these will be the focus of the remainder of the chapter.

PHYSICAL ENVIRONMENT

In practice, both sides generally agree to the negotiation site, usually an education center or a school library. If possible, carefully evaluating and recommending other locations for the sessions may lead to a beneficial change for all parties involved in the negotiations. A volunteer from each team may wish to conduct an investigation into the availability of facilities. Having them visit the sites together, discuss the pros and cons of each, and make recommendations to each side may be the beginning of successful negotiations sessions.

Possible sites to consider include banks, meeting rooms in office buildings, private banquet rooms, and clubhouses where the settings are neutral and centrally located. Many organizations are very willing to share their facilities at no cost, and a few may provide refreshments. However, if teachers are planning to picket a site during negotiations, using these locations may not be a good idea for obvious reasons.

When selecting the conference facility, spatial organization, size, seating arrangement, lighting, color, temperature, noise, and accessibility should be considered. Physical comfort of negotiators is paramount because discomfort may negatively affect the attitudes of people under pressure. Even room color and attractiveness are important environmental considerations, as researchers have determined that environmental aesthetics influence behavior and communication.[2]

A cluttered environment sends the wrong message; too large a room may diminish the importance of the tasks at hand or suggest the insignificance of the negotiators. Even dirty restroom facilities can send the wrong message. Hearing repeated school announcements at the close of the day can be more than a little distracting and possibly enough justification not to hold meetings in schools when they are in session. Certainly rooms with buzzing fluorescent lights have a negative affect on moods and can negatively impact the sessions.

Table arrangements in negotiations may send subliminal messages. Although the best arrangement depends on the situation, some foster trust and closeness. For example, having members seated at a round table generally is the most conducive to open and honest dialogue, because of the equality conveyed. However, depending on the number of participants in negotiations, this arrangement might not be feasible. And if a negotiating team wishes to convey power and authority, they may opt for a different arrangement.

Typically, each side will sit along a rectangular table facing each other. The wider the tables, obviously, the more distance between the opposing sides. Although subtle, this arrangement may convey a feeling of more than physical distance. A comfortable distance from the opposing side would be approximately four to twelve feet. If the distance is less than four feet, some negotiators may become uncomfortable as their "personal space" is invaded and the distance reserved for interpersonal contact or intimacy is approached.

The tables should provide enough space for each person to be seated comfortably and have room for papers, laptops, or other items. The tables and chairs should be free from defects, such as splinters or rough edges that tend to snag knits or stockings. Some tables provide the appropriate connections for Internet access; some negotiators may relish being able to use a modem to access much needed information or communicate with others during appropriate times. This may be especially true if obtaining the latest information from another source is critical during negotiations.

Usually, the chief negotiator sits in the center of one side of the table, which sends a message of authority and an image of a unified negotiation team. This placement also assists other team members in being able to communicate with the negotiator by passing notes, providing cues, or occasionally whispering relevant information. Being aware of any glare in the room and positioning appropriately is strongly recommended. Some negotiators prefer to be seated on the side of the table facing an exit. The central negotiator should have enough room on either side of him or her so that if the negotiator wants to make a key point while standing, he or she can do so easily.

This is not done often, although some negotiators do attempt to gain an advantage on the other side by standing when making key points or by appearing physically higher by other means. For example, negotiators have been known to raise their chairs above the height of those on the other side, just as some school boards will sit at tables on raised platforms while visitors must "look up" to address the members. Sometimes the purpose of this elevation is not just for better observation of the participants. A case in point would be the elevation of a judge's bench.

PERSONAL ATTRIBUTES

Physical Appearance

Personal attributes include physical appearance, vocal cues, and touch. Physical appearance refers to attributes of image such as sex, race, height, weight, body shape, hairstyle, dress, artifacts, and attractiveness. Considering that Americans spend billions of dollars annually on cosmetics, cosmetic surgery, and weight-loss programs, the importance of physical appearance cannot be denied. Furthermore, recent studies have supported what has long been assumed regarding the advantages of being attractive.

Research indicates that more attractive people have a definite advantage in securing employment, earning more money, appearing more influential, and receiving preferential treatment.

Several television journalists have conducted investigations into the effects of physical appearance when trying to secure employment or obtain assistance with a flat tire. Interviewees for a job were paired with a less attractive person of the same sex who appeared to have the same skills, education, and qualifications, and who dressed similarly; in every case, the more attractive person had the advantage. The same results were replicated with persons trying to obtain assistance with a flat tire. These and similar studies have revealed the importance of attractiveness in being influential, although the ramifications have led to much controversy. The possible implications of selecting some team members based on physical appearance in negotiations should be considered very carefully.

Researchers have found that the way one dresses influences perceptions of attractiveness, popularity, self-esteem, social power, and income level, and has the most powerful affect on credibility. In a situation in which one intends to be powerful, the importance of dressing for success should not be overlooked. Many successful women refer to wearing a "power suit" when conducting important business, negotiating, or interviewing. Even when negotiations are conducted in the summer or in the evening and the atmosphere is more relaxed, casual dress may reduce the nonverbal emphasis on credibility and professionalism.

Therefore, considering the importance of credibility and social power, a wise negotiator should consider wearing something similar to what he or she would wear to an interview or if expecting a promotion. However, if members of the other team are wearing jeans and sports outfits during negotiations, too formal an appearance can set up a barrier to good communications because the negotiator may be viewed as too rigid or distant. In this case, a negotiator might want to adopt a slightly less formal dress code, but still be aware of the message being sent by any deviation from his or her normal way of dressing for success.

In terms of accessories, jewelry should be kept to a minimum. Even today, some people are offended by men wearing bracelets and "pinkie rings," and this could be enough reason to save that jewelry for other occasions. Too much makeup can also lessen one's credibility.

Although wearing cologne or perfume is a matter of personal prefer-ence, a negotiator should be aware that others may be allergic to or of-fended by certain fragrances. Of course, gum chewing can be dis-tracting and is certainly not conducive to being viewed as influential. Needless to say, smoking should never be attempted or allowed in any negotiation room.

Vocal Cues

Vocal or speech cues convey more than the words being stated. The frequency and duration of speech during a fixed period of communi-cation as well as the greater tendency to interrupt others are good in-dicators of dominance. A skilled negotiator should be cognizant of the amount of time his team, compared with the other team, is engaged in verbal communication. While the negotiator does not want to dom-inate all verbal interactions, he should be aware of when the other team begins to dominate consistently and then take appropriate ac-tions to regain his position.

Varying the volume during negotiations can lead to dramatic effects. For example, a male negotiator might wish to use a slightly louder voice, as louder speech is considered more persuasive and more influ-ential; a higher-pitched voice and slower rate of speech are judged as more submissive or deceitful. At other times, the negotiator may want to lower his voice almost to a whisper to make a point. Silence, too, can send a strong message.

A regular, rhythmic voice pattern suggests confidence, while vocal or speech cues to avoid include a nasal voice, which can be annoying, and a monotone, which suggests apathy or boredom. An excessive rate of speech may be perceived as an indicator of nervousness and may in-crease the perception of intensity, while frequent pauses or a slow rate of speech may be frustrating to the listener. Repetition of words, except when making points, stuttering, and not enunciating clearly are viewed negatively; mispronouncing words may suggest ignorance or incompe-tence. After investigating implicit speech clues that were most likely to accompany deceit, Mehrabian concluded that speech errors, halting speech, and tremors in the voice were found more frequently in deceit-ful than in truthful communication.

Touch

Since negotiations can begin and end with a handshake, nonverbal messages can be sent in this act and can have a significant effect on perceptions. A firm handshake generally conveys positive attributes: more intensity, a greater likability, and a warmer feeling than a loose handshake, which can convey weakness, aloofness, unwillingness, unfriendliness, and lack of affection. A handshake that is vice-like may suggest intimidation, while forcefully shaking up and down too much is considered rude and excessive. One that is too prolonged in most cases is considered unacceptable—invasive and too intimate.

The use of the appropriate handshake in negotiations can bring about positive change. For example, when each side is introduced, a firm handshake sends a positive message. Although handshakes are generally not used at the end of each session, walking over to members of the other negotiating team and shaking hands after a difficult session might be an effective tool in de-escalating tensions and conveying a willingness to continue further negotiations at a later date. A technique used to send a positive message would be briefly prolonging the handshake, grasping the forearm or upper arm of the other person, or using encouraging words during the handshake.

BODY LANGUAGE

Body language includes, but is not limited to, facial expressions, body movements, gestures, postures, eye contact, and positioning in a group. Since body language tends to be involuntary, a skillful negotiator can deduce a wealth of information when observing members on the opposing negotiation team. Being aware of ways to use body language to communicate and doing so effectively can be an invaluable skill, especially during negotiations.

The significance and implications of understanding and using body language have been demonstrated by the work of Milton Erickson, considered by many to be the master of hypnotherapy. Dr. Erickson was born with deficient color vision, tone deafness, no sense of rhythm, and dyslexia;

he also suffered from attacks of poliomyelitis at ages seventeen and fifty-one. During his first attack, after being in a coma for three days, he was paralyzed although he retained his vision and could move his eyes and speak with great difficulty. During his recovery, he would play mental games, listening to sounds such as the barn door opening and footsteps, to identify the person making them. Through these exercises, he became a skilled observer and communicator, as he gathered information from body language. He became extremely powerful in his therapeutic sessions because of his knowledge and application of nonverbal communication.

The study of body movement is also known as "kinesics," a term derived from the Greek word for movement and referring to all body movements except for touching. Whether interpreting or sending nonverbal messages, one is advised to consider the overall communication patterns, especially when conflicting information is present. For example, a wink could signal flirtation or reveal a nervous twitch, an irritating contact lens, or an allergy. A negotiator might state in a very controlled and authoritative voice that the current proposal is the best that will be offered, but his seated body may convey other messages by his rapidly tapping foot and by his eyes blinking frequently and not focusing on the listeners. His words may be deceitful, he might be stressed from prolonged negotiations, he could be worried that if this final attempt fails he has nothing to offer, or he may be fearful of returning to his constituents with no agreement. More information would be needed to accurately assess his nonverbal messages.

After carefully observing him for several days previously, a member of the opposing team might have noticed that, in the afternoons, the negotiator had a tendency not to look at the other team when speaking, especially immediately after lunch. The member also may have noticed and possibly was annoyed that the negotiator always tapped his foot, even when eating. But the member has not previously noticed the negotiator's frequent eye blinking, exhibited now as he makes his statement about the current proposal. This behavior may therefore demonstrate deception or dishonesty. Looking away while speaking or quick, sideways glances can indicate the same. As a result of such observations, additional evidence revealing patterns of behavior provides valuable clues to interpreting a negotiator's body language.

Sometimes, careful evaluation of the topics at hand may be indicated by peering out over eyeglasses, cupping the chin between thumb and fingers, putting the thumb under the chin and the index finger to the cheek, placing the hands to the bridge of the nose, or stroking the chin. When the negotiator observes these indicators from the other team members after he has presented items for consideration, he may surmise that his points are being evaluated. Likewise, if he engages in any of these behaviors after hearing opposing arguments, he is sending the signal that he is considering those items discussed. Conversely, if he were to place his head in his hands and not look at the speaker, he may be indicating indifference, boredom, or an unwillingness to mediate items being enumerated.

Most negotiators are aware that facial expressions denote emotions such as happiness, sadness, surprise, bewilderment, interest, fear, anger, disgust, contempt, and determination, and that these expressions change frequently during negotiations. Through a series of experiments, Mehrabian concluded that "total feeling = 7% verbal feeling + 38% vocal feeling + 55% facial feeling." In other words, his results revealed that the impact of facial expression was greater than vocal expression, which was greater than the spoken word. Furthermore, when facial expressions and words were incongruous, he found that facial expressions prevailed and determined the impact of the message.[3] His findings confirm the importance of negotiators observing facial expressions and matching their own body movements to their verbal communications.

Leathers has noted positive types of gestures that enhance credibility perceptions. These include using gestures to add emphasis when making points, signaling a desire to speak, or encouraging someone else to speak. He believes that gestures should be spontaneous, relaxed, and unrehearsed. The hands and arms should be kept away from the body to increase their persuasive impact. Gestures should indicate feelings or emotion.[4]

Some gestures give the appearance of being defensive, nervous, and lacking confidence. These include tugging at clothing, lip licking, hand wringing, finger tapping, biting fingernails, constant fidgeting, chewing on a pencil, out of context smiling, grimacing, and covering the mouth with the hand while speaking—the last one indicating deception or dishonesty. Mehrabian found that deceitful people often nod and gesture less, exhibit less frequent leg and foot movement while seated, increase self-manipulation such as scratching the head or touching other body parts, show a vigilant or tense quality of movement and speech, and smile more if not anxious.[5] Other gestures indicating deception include frequent swallowing and throat clearing.

The last nonverbal message to be reviewed is postural relaxation, which is significant in terms of the degree of symmetry of the body in a standing or sitting position. For example, compare the symmetry of a soldier standing at attention with that of one who is leaning to one side with one hand in his pocket, head somewhat to the side, and talking to a friend. Or notice the difference between a student in a somewhat re-clining position with legs crossed in a chair and one leaning forward with shoulders fairly erect. Nonverbal messages are being conveyed in each of these positions.

Leaning forward in response to a question may establish rapport, while tilting the head toward the speaker or sitting on the edge of the chair can indicate interest. While speaking, responsiveness can be indi-cated by frequent and forceful postural shifts. Negative postural indica-tors include crossed arms high on the chest, sloppy or informal body posture, body tension, rigidity, or a timid and constricted posture.

Studies have revealed that postural relaxation is a subtle indicator of social dominance, and that dominant people assume a relaxed posture while submissive people assume a less-relaxed or tenser posture. In ad-dition, communicators in more relaxed positions tend to be viewed as more influential in eliciting opinion change. It has been noted that peo-ple in inferior positions often lower their heads more, while individuals of higher status often look at others for a greater duration.

A successful negotiator may want to utilize this information on the message transmitted by posture and monitor his or her own posture. He may want to observe other team members to determine the state of relaxation demonstrated. If his team members appear to be stressed, he may wish to take a recess and share the importance of ap-pearing relaxed. Learning and practicing relaxation techniques can be advantageous. Encouraging team members to engage in activities that relieve stress outside of the sessions during the negotiation period is recommended.

CONCLUSION

This chapter has provided only a brief review of nonverbal communication. The importance of observing, monitoring, and controlling these cues cannot be overemphasized during the negotiation process. This is especially true when negotiations involve deceptions. When nonverbal cues and spoken messages are incongruous, miscommunication often occurs and serious errors in strategies can result in unsuitable contracts. Conversely, navigating difficult sessions successfully may be a result of accurately utilizing nonverbal cues. Therefore, a wise negotiator should become well acquainted with current research and the implications inherent in nonverbal communication.

SUMMARY

This chapter presented information and research on how nonverbal communication can be useful to the negotiator. The successful negotiator should be able to examine the physical environment, look at the personal attributes of the members of both negotiating teams, and observe body language to see what people are saying without using any words. The second part of the next chapter will introduce the concept of win–win negotiations, in which both teams try to arrive at a contractual agreement without the traditional adversarial bargaining. The information in the current chapter can be used in both kinds of bargaining. For example, you can use the information about physical surroundings and apparel to make everyone comfortable for win–win bargaining. Or you can use the same information to give yourself and your team an advantage in traditional bargaining.

NOTES

1. M. Hickson and D. Stacks, *Nonverbal Communication: Studies and Applications*, 3d ed. (Madison, Wis.: WCB Brown & Benchmark, 1993), 5.

2. N. L. Mintz, "Effects of Esthetic Surroundings, II: Prolonged and Repeated Experience in a 'Beautiful' and 'Ugly Room,'" *Journal of Psychology* 41 (1956), 459–66.

3. A. Mehrabian, *Silent Messages: Implicit Communication of Emotions and Attitudes,* 2d ed. (Belmont, Calif.: Wadsworth, 1981), 76–77.

4. D. G. Leathers, "The Role of Nonverbal Factors in Shaping Perceptions of Leadership" (seminar presented at the University of Southern Mississippi, Hattiesburg, Miss., 1982).

5. Mehrabian, *Silent Messages,* 153.

8

WIN–WIN BARGAINING AND OTHER APPROACHES TO BARGAINING

Clete R. Bulach and Karen M. Moriarty

This book has concentrated on the traditional approach to collective bargaining, an approach that came from the private sector and is still used in most school districts that bargain with their teachers.

There are other ways to arrive at a contract, however, and this chapter discusses some of these alternate approaches.

Two educators were asked to contribute to this chapter because of their specific experiences. The first part, written by Clete Bulach, gives an overall historical perspective, describes various approaches to bargaining, tells why they have evolved, and gives Bulach's opinions on these different approaches.

The latter part of this chapter, written by Karen Moriarty, describes one specific approach and tells how her district used this approach successfully to reach an agreement. A brief note following Moriarty's contribution discusses survey research on win–win bargaining. The notes at the end of the chapter mostly apply to the section written by Bulach.

Both parts of this chapter were updated from an earlier edition by the book's author to add recent research. The basic content has not been changed.

THE COLLECTIVE BARGAINING POTPOURRI: IS THERE A RIGHT WAY?

Clete R. Bulach

During the 1960s and 1970s, the rules for collective bargaining were easy to understand. The teachers had their list of demands and went to the table to see how many of them they could get without having to resort to a strike to get them. The board and administration, likewise, had their list, and they went to the table to see how many they could get in return for what they were willing to give. Sometimes the board and administration were unwilling to give what the teachers felt they had to have and a strike resulted. Teachers had to be prepared to strike, and boards had to be prepared to defend against a strike.

It was an extremely adversarial relationship. If you were a superintendent or board member, you could expect to be personally attacked. In the event of a strike, picket lines, where professional teachers sometimes became very unprofessional, would be put in place to deter students and employees from going to school. A media war would follow in the papers and television, as each side tried to win the support of the public. Eventually, one side or both sides would give something they said they never would, or one side would get tired, and the strike would end.

During the 1980s, collective bargaining underwent many changes. Instead of the traditional approach, other strategies were being used, for example, the "dual collective bargaining,"[1] "integrative bargaining,"[2] "cooperative bargaining,"[3] and "win–win bargaining"[4] strategies. Each of these strategies has its advocates, with win–win bargaining and traditional bargaining being the most popular.

What has brought about this change in the bargaining process? Is there a best strategy to employ at the bargaining table? To answer these questions, the author will review the literature on collective bargaining and draw on his own experience as a negotiator on both sides of the table. First, the reasons why these changes have occurred will be analyzed. Next, each of the different bargaining strategies will be described. Finally, the pros and cons of and rules for using the various strategies will be described to see if there is a best strategy for collective bargaining.

The changes in the bargaining process from the private-sector, industrial model to the currently evolving models have been caused by three factors: mature labor contracts, costly labor disputes, and the rising cry of teacher empowerment.

Many school districts have been negotiating with employee unions since the 1960s. The end results of all these years of negotiations are very mature contracts that cover all aspects of what has traditionally been held to be a subject of collective bargaining, that is, money, fringe benefits, and working conditions (old areas). As a result, unions have attempted to move into new areas, for example, the policy area, because the language in the contract in the old areas was what they wanted. Consequently, the union's negotiation package contained items that previously had been left to board policy.

Geisert calls these new areas, such as curriculum, committee memberships, and selection of instructional materials, the professional areas.[5] These are categorized as more complex issues that were not found to lend themselves to formal negotiations. A more cooperative form of bargaining was necessary to deal with problems in the policy domain.[6] Consequently, because some unions had mature contracts and needed new areas to put on their laundry lists, and because these new areas did not lend themselves to resolution via traditional collective bargaining, new models have evolved.

As long as the traditional model worked and resulted in contracts between the employer and the employee union, its continued use was assured. However, when it didn't work, at heavy costs to both the employer and the employee union, they began looking for other methods or models to settle contract negotiations. According to Moriarty, one of the most noticeable characteristics of districts that sent attendees to a workshop on "Win–Win Collective Bargaining" was labor strife and unrest in recent years.[7] Others, such as Hansen[8] and Cox and Stevens,[9] also describe districts with a history of labor conflict as turning to win–win collective bargaining.

These districts were dissatisfied with the traditional method of collective bargaining because the costs far outweighed the gains. Labor strife, job actions, strikes, mistrust, hard feelings, poor public relations for board members and the school district, and degradation of the professional image of the teachers are some of the costs of the traditional method when it doesn't work. Whenever both sides realized that the costs incurred far outweighed the gains, they began looking for new methods for collective bargaining.

The third factor that has heavily influenced the move away from the traditional method of collective bargaining is a series of reports dealing with the need for education reform. The Carnegie Forum, the Holmes Group, and the Conley and Bacharach reports all called for the empowerment of teachers as one of the ways to reform education. With this impetus, unions and others began the movement to involve teachers in the decision-making process, thereby empowering them. Jamieson and Jurist,[10] Lucas,[11] and Namit and Swift[12] all describe the involvement of teachers in the problem-solving/decision-making process as a part of collective bargaining. Peck states that the trend is to use collective bargaining to secure a role for teachers in decision making.[13] The movement to empower teachers and involve them in the decision-making process was fueled by the preceding reports and influenced the popularity of the win–win approach, and variations thereof, as opposed to traditional collective bargaining techniques.

The present collective bargaining strategies being used across the United States seem to fall somewhere on a continuum, ranging from the traditional method on one end to a narrow version of win–win on the other end. The traditional method, in addition to the description given in the opening of this section of the chapter, is characterized by:

- the hiring of a chief negotiator who is not an employee of the school district and the absence of board members at the bargaining table;[14]
- union concern for the welfare and protection of union members;[15]
- the absence of the superintendent from the collective bargaining team;[16]
- the use of power tactics on both sides of the table;[17] and
- an adversarial process.[18]

The win–win approach, described by Moriarty in its most restrictive form, is characterized by:

- the recommendation of the leadership of both parties to use the win–win strategy;

- both sides adopting a clearly articulated value system, for example, each side valuing the survival and good of the district;
- the hiring of a neutral facilitator who is skilled in mediations to oversee the process;
- the formal adoption of rules, by both sides, that will govern the process;
- all members of the board and the superintendent serving on the negotiating team;
- the large size of the negotiating teams (usually ten or more people to a team);
- the formation of subcommittees within the teams to study problems that can't be resolved easily;
- marathon sessions on weekends; and
- a mutual commitment to settling the contract on a preestablished date and within a thirty-day time period.[19]

There are many variations on the preceding two processes. One of the more interesting involves both processes used in a negotiations process, depending on the item that is being bargained. Namit and Swift call this "dual collective bargaining."[20] They distinguish between bargaining and problem solving. The traditional items, for example, money, fringe benefits, and working conditions, are dealt with in the traditional bargaining method; all other areas are dealt with in a collaborative problem-solving process. Others such as Geisert have also recommended this dual approach to the bargaining process.[21]

One of the earlier variations of the win–win bargaining process was called "informal negotiations." Adair describes a school district that, because of hard-nosed negotiations in the past, "was ripe for a better way of settling teacher contract talks." The teachers' team was selected by the school board from a list of teachers who were willing to be on the team. The board team was selected by the teachers from a list supplied by the board. Neither team had a spokesperson. Everyone on either team was to engage in a free exchange of ideas in an informal setting. Game playing, jockeying for position, and insincere demands were to be replaced by openness and trust. Each team would make its first offer its best offer, and each team would accept the other's offer as such. It was further agreed that, if agreement could not be reached, informal negotiations would end and formal negotiations would commence. Agreement was reached, however, and the teams further agreed to reconvene informal negotiations if other items were raised during the year.[22]

Huber and Hennies describe a variation of win–win in their formula for positive and productive contract talks. They list "five guiding lights":

- work toward a common goal, for example, excellence in education;
- agree on school finances, hiring a teacher whom both sides can trust to study the district's finances;
- help each other win;
- keep communications open; and
- develop a trusting relationship.[23]

This oversimplifies the approach with the intent to show that it is a much less restrictive approach to win–win bargaining.

Another variation on win–win is called "integrative bargaining." According to Schachter, during one negotiations process, when teachers "became frustrated at the impasses they reached with the traditional process, they set about trying to devise structures that would support a more integrative, win–win stance."

Schachter indicates that there is no distinct line between traditional bargaining and integrative bargaining, but he does suggest four distinct changes:

- use no professional outside negotiators—the people at the table have to have a stake in the outcome;
- hold frequent year-round meetings—deal with problems as they come up and don't wait until the contract expires;
- open communication—no hidden agendas and no "throwaway" items; and
- use a problem-solving approach—try to solve problems rather than win points.[24]

As can be seen from the preceding, many districts around the country are using variations of the traditional and win–win approaches to collective bargaining. Is one of the approaches a best approach? Further analysis will be required before this question can be answered.

Critics of the traditional approach are far more numerous than those of the win–win approach, but the win–win critics do raise some valid concerns. Critics of the traditional approach see it as an "I win–you lose" approach. According to Schachter, "To ensure victory, participants withhold information, procrastinate, and add or subtract irrelevant demands, thus giving a phony appearance of moving toward compromise. Process values such as honesty and openness are less important to a side than getting its items in the final package. Union leader Albert Shanker summed up the model's conflictual premises by saying, Power is taken from someone. Teachers . . . are now starting to take power from supervisors and school boards.'"[25]

Some describe the traditional process as a battle. Bishop states that after many years of action and reaction, threats and counterthreats, and alienation on all sides, it should be clear that traditional bargaining is a failure. Further, he states that we need to move away from a history of combative, destructive bargaining because it has resulted in low morale, hostility, poor communications, reduced cooperation, inhibited change, minimized achievement, increased frustration, and confusion for everyone.[26]

While the win–win approach has many advocates, it also has its critics. Lieberman states that the goal of collective bargaining is not and should not be to achieve labor peace and harmony, if it is at the expense of management rights. He further states that "generous school systems raise teacher expectations and thus have more—not fewer—labor problems" because they create "a level of expectation that is hard to satisfy."[27] In another article, Lieberman states that teachers' unions exist solely to protect the employees and are unwilling to monitor their own membership and hold incompetent and unethical teachers accountable.[28] Abel tends to support this position.[29] Lieberman is not so much a critic of win–win as he is of the role teacher unions play in the bargaining process. Kearney adds that teachers' unions need to support causes besides wages and working conditions. They should admit when they have taken incorrect positions and should take leadership roles in establishing procedures to reduce violence in their schools and to support national, state, and local academic standards.[30] If one agrees with Lieberman, one could hardly support win–win because one of its essential ingredients is trust.[31] It would appear that Lieberman is saying that teachers' unions are not to be trusted.

Others such as Van Wilkinson believe that participatory management, which is defined as "an organizational system wherein non-management employees formally share in the decision-making processes" must go hand in hand with participatory responsibility. Wilkinson doesn't see this happening because there is little self-policing done by teachers.[32]

Geisert believes that the new movement of empowering teachers by involving them in the decision-making process is a disguise for union empowerment rather than an attempt at professionalizing teachers. He believes that the school board holds a public trust and cannot give up control of the school's system. And the further teachers move into the decision-making process, the less significant the board and the administration become. Geisert is not so much opposed to involving teachers in the decision-making process as he is opposed to involving teacher unions in the process. He states: "Perhaps traditional collective bargaining has outlived its usefulness. But as long as teacher unions retain an adversarial trade-union approach to bargaining that seeks conformity, uniformity, and seniority for union members, it is oxymoronic to speak of a professional approach to unionism."[33]

Shedd believes that collective bargaining in public education is changing such that relationships are becoming more cooperative. But he cautions that it will not always be harmonious. He believes that the parties involved will always have different perspectives on what their clients need, as well as different priorities. He sees "a scrappy new form of unionism [that] is already being delivered naturally by 'traditional' collective bargaining itself—while most observers are looking for the stork to deliver a little bundle of love."[34] Kearney states, "The traditional union determination to limit management discretion and authority through restrictive contract language and grievance procedures appears to be increasingly out of step with the needs of competent, and particularly high-performance organizations."[35] With today's emphasis on standards and the public's desire for better schools and for reform efforts, teacher unions need to rethink their positions on restrictive contract language and make more of an effort to work with the administration on these issues.

Rist tries to sort out the pros and cons of the new movement of empowering teachers. She indicates that, in some circles, teacher empowerment is the most significant development in education in this country, while in others it is the most clever tactic ever devised by unions to get, in the name of school improvement, what they couldn't get in the name of unionization. She interviewed a number of school executives and concluded that many of them back away from teacher empowerment when it becomes entangled with union empowerment. She concludes on a positive note: "Democracy, in school systems as elsewhere, is messy. . . . Yet that very messiness is a by-product of a process that can release energy and excitement among teachers and parents in your schools. And such energy and excitement, empowerment proponents maintain, can put your schools on the track to success."[36]

This positive quote provides a good transition to the positive aspects of the traditional and win–win approaches to collective bargaining. Despite the previous criticisms, each approach and all the variations in between do have a lot of positive aspects. The traditional approach has worked successfully for many years and continues to work well in many districts.

According to Eiler, the traditional approach is a viable collective bargaining model, provided that the negotiators understand the process and follow certain guidelines. If these guidelines, which he calls "golden rules," are followed, the end result will be a successful labor contract. His rules for the negotiating teams are:

1. Be patient.
2. Be succinct.
3. Know where to begin.
4. Don't shoot yourself in the foot.
5. Agree on some ground rules.
6. Don't be afraid to say, "No!"
7. Show flexibility during talks.
8. Learn how important different issues are and to whom they are important.
9. Don't overdo contract talks.
10. Avoid personal attacks.
11. Foster a problem-solving mentality.
12. Be forgiving of mistakes.

His rules for the members of the board of education are:

1. Be patient.
2. Be aware of new bargaining issues.
3. Don't worry too much about money.

4. Don't appeal directly to the union membership.
5. Don't make private commitments.
6. Support your negotiators.
7. Keep quiet on bargaining issues.
8. Seek out principals' support.
9. Put experts on your team.
10. Be wary of outside parties.
11. Avoid unfair labor practices.
12. Remember your first responsibility, which is to the children of the school district.[37]

This author subscribes to the preceding ground rules, but would add one. It is extremely important that neither side in the negotiations process be perceived by the other side as the winner. Should this occur, then the stage is set for the next time, when the other side, perceiving they have lost, will be determined to even the score. They will attempt to structure their negotiations package so they will be the winners. After all, in the case of the teachers, for instance, they have an obligation to their membership to show them that they are getting something for their dues. Should the teachers be successful and be seen as the winners, then the board and administrators will try to even the score in the next round; and so it will go until both sides have their backs against the wall and are unwilling to give one more iota, lest they be perceived by their membership as the loser again. Given this scenario, the stage is set for impasse and a possible strike.

To summarize this last point, the end result of the traditional bargaining process is to have it appear that both negotiation teams have won, thereby resulting in a win–win situation. If this is not possible, the next preferred situation is to have it appear that neither side won, thereby resulting in a lose–lose situation. The least-preferred situation is a win–lose situation, because it only sets the stage for poor labor-management relations, hard feelings, and a "Just wait until the next time!" mentality.

Is there a positive outcome to the lose–lose situation? It is the opinion of this author and others[38] that both sides, after repeated lose–lose situations, are ready to try different methods of bargaining, for example, win–win bargaining.

There are many positive aspects to win–win bargaining, provided that a few ground rules are followed. Parts of these ground rules can be found scattered throughout this section of the chapter. Suggested ground rules consist of agreement by both sides on:

1. Who and how many people should be on each team.
2. The use of an outside consultant to provide several weekends of training for both bargaining teams prior to the start of the bargaining process in such areas as interpersonal communications, problem solving and decision making, goal setting, conflict management, and trust development. This time should also be used to come to agreement on items 3–8 below. Rationale: (1) this will facilitate the development of openness and trust that is essential to the win–win process; (2) this will provide both teams with the skill they will need to deal with the process; (3) coming to agreement on items 3–8 provides a good opportunity for the consultant to give each person feedback on their use of the aforementioned skills; and (4) these two weekends serve as a warm-up for the negotiations process and provide both sides with enough information to decide whether to continue with the win–win process or revert back to the traditional process. One sure indication that the teams are not ready to proceed with the win–win process is a failure to agree on items 3–8.
3. A set of goals or values; for example, decisions of the teams shall be guided by the benefit of those decisions to students, the school district, the employees, and/or the community, in that order of priority. For example, no decision should be made that benefits teachers and harms students, as would be the case if too much of the budget went for salaries and delayed adoption of a new reading text due to insufficient funds.
4. The use of outside personnel in the bargaining process. None should be used on either team! They may be used as observers or advisers, but they should not sit at the table. Rationale: (1) this is a local matter for local personnel; (2) the fear of union empowerment is lessened if the involvement of outside personnel is lessened; and (3) this is one of the few areas in which trust can be demonstrated; that is, the greater the level of trust, the less the need for outside personnel.

5. Board members are observers only and at least one must be present at all sessions. Rationale: (1) board members have neither the expertise nor the working relationship with teachers to negotiate a contract and (2) the presence of at least one board member as an observer is helpful in informing other board members of the progress or lack of progress that is being made;

6. When to communicate with the news media and who does the communicating (members of the employee organization, members of the board, someone else?).

7. The use of one principal on the board team who represents each level of the district's organizational structure. Rationale: the building principals are the ones who will administer the contract. There will be fewer contract administration problems if the people who have to deal with the contract on a day-to-day basis help to negotiate and write it.

8. The ongoing use of the win–win process to deal with nonmonetary problems as they arise. Rationale: empowering teachers and involving them in the decision-making process has to be done on a continual basis and not every two or three years when a new contract has to be negotiated.

Kearney agrees with this last point when he says that administrators today seem to be more willing to work cooperatively with teacher unions than they have been in the past. Also, administrators have been trained to know about concepts like shared decision making. In the same way, teachers' unions have to do their parts in cooperating with administrators and not automatically assuming the adversarial role.[39] The author of this book (Sharp) once assumed a new superintendency in a district that had had three strikes in four years. He suggested to the teachers' union president that they meet periodically for breakfast or lunch to discuss concerns before they became problems or formal grievances and to develop trust between the union and the administration. The union president agreed to the meetings and then added, "We can never trust you because you are the superintendent." The title "superintendent" alone meant that he could not be trusted by the union leadership. As Kearny says, "A strong adversarial spirit still prevails in most unionized jurisdictions."[40]

The use of the win–win process will result in different decision-making structures for each district. Some districts will follow that of Boston City Schools,[41] where teachers and parents are given responsibility for decisions at the building-site level. Others will involve committees at the district level. Some may involve parents and students and others will not.

Anyone wishing for information on different decision-making structures could consult school systems that have implemented site-based decision making (SBDM), for example, school districts in Kentucky that have been under state mandate to implement SBDM since 1991; school districts in Dade County, Florida; and Boston City Schools. However, the reader should be cautioned that SBDM "is only one way to restructure decision making and planning at the school site so that day-to-day administration and teaching can be collaborative and collegial."[42] Taylor and Levine suggest the effective schools movement as another source for finding ways to involve parents and teachers in the decision-making process.

To summarize, there really doesn't appear to be a best method or process for collective bargaining. The process that will be most effective will depend on the history and culture of the school district, its success or lack of success with the traditional process, and the trends at the local level for teacher empowerment and involvement in the decision-making process. The traditional process will work best in those districts where it has been successful, where management has been somewhat autocratic, where outside professional negotiators are a strong force, and where there is no desire to empower teachers. Conversely, where there has been a history of problems with the traditional process, where participatory management is practiced, where outside professional negotiators can be removed from the process, and where there is a desire to empower teachers, then win–win bargaining is the best process.

WIN–WIN BARGAINING: THIRTY DAYS TO A CONTRACT

Karen M. Moriarty

"Flight planning"—setting your destination before beginning—is a key concept in win–win bargaining. A mutual commitment to settling on a preestablished date—within thirty days—should be made by the board and the union through the assistance of a neutral facilitator.

Another required ingredient of win–win negotiations is the adoption by both sides of a clearly articulated value system. Adopting this set of values is different from the traditional, adversarial model of bargaining. According to the Goldaber model of win–win, traditional bargaining has been based upon an international model of opposing values between the sides. In contrast, the win–win model incorporates an intranational model with shared goals, in this case, the survival and good of the district. Sociologist Goldaber draws an analogy to the sports model in which team owners, recognizing the good of the league as the priority in their planning and decision making, cooperate and never lose focus upon this shared value. It is the fans in the seats or bleachers who play out the adversarial role that is characteristic of the international model: the fans want the defeat of the other team. While the owners simulate the win–win model as proposed by Irving Goldaber, the fans' behavior and direction are analogous to some of the behaviors that are characteristic of the win–lose mentality in traditional collective bargaining. (However, the baseball negotiations of 2002 nearly united fans on both sides against both the owners and the players, as both seemed to lose sight of any "shared value.")

The values inherent in win–win bargaining, as well as the advantages and disadvantages of this approach, would be appropriate and interesting topics for a separate article, but this section of this chapter will describe the process of the win–win model as it was utilized in Illinois District 230.

In late winter, the district superintendent, controller, assistant superintendent for personnel, two board members, and three teacher negotiations team members attended a win–win workshop conducted by Goldaber. The three-day workshop, held from Thursday through Saturday morning, provided an orientation to the values of the model, the model's process, and its protocols. Present at the workshop were representatives from several districts—administrators and union leaders—in which the approach had been recently utilized successfully. The most notable shared characteristic of the districts was the labor strife and unrest that had been experienced in recent years, in one case exhibited by a thirty-one day strike and more than one year of unsuccessful court-ordered bargaining.

By Saturday at noon, the eight participants from District 230 were ready to recommend to their respective constituencies the adoption of this model for the teacher contract that was due to expire in the summer. During the coming days and weeks, several meetings were held to discuss the potential merits of win–win bargaining for the district.

Dr. Goldaber, who agreed to serve as the required neutral facilitator, came to meet for two hours with the board of education and key administrators and for another two hours with the teachers' association representatives. After these meetings, the two sides were willing to make a commitment to the win–win process.

Following this decision, a number of significant events occurred to prepare for the success of the bargaining process. First, the "flight planning" was effected as the projected ratification date of the contract was set by both sides—the board and the association. Two required weekends were set so that calendars could be cleared and arrangements made for the extensive negotiations sessions. Information was readily and openly shared, including the financial records of the district and other assorted data related to the district and its employees, for example, current salary and experiential data, the budget, audit, and enrollment and economic projections for the next two-plus years.

The formal adoption of forty-eight win–win protocols, that is, rules that would govern the entire process, was undertaken by both the board and the association. These written protocols had been recommended by Goldaber, but were modified based upon the wishes of the board and association negotiations teams. The most significant change was the addition of a protocol regarding communications with the media during the bargaining process. It was agreed that all communications would come from the board president and the association president jointly throughout the course of the thirty-day period. This protocol emphasizes the unique nature of the win–win process and also symbolizes its "highly civilized" and cooperative mode—as the board and association presidents characterized win–win negotiations for the local media after its successful resolution.

Another significant departure from more traditional bargaining is the condition that the entire board become directly involved in negotiating the contract with the teachers' association team. All seven members of the board participated in negotiations with all seven members of the association team. Three resource persons for each team were also directly involved—the superintendent, the assistant superintendent for personnel, and the controller from the administration on behalf of the board and the association president, along with Illinois Education Association UniServ director and a district teacher for the teachers' team. (This aspect of the process might serve as the topic for another article, and could be the subject of controversy because of the pervasiveness and intensity of the process and the time commitment required of all twenty persons.)

On the weekend of June 1, all twenty participants and the facilitator met in a comfortable, quiet, and neutral place—a room at the local community college student center—for Friday evening, all day Saturday, and Sunday morning. The purpose of the weekend was to discuss all matters related to the district, the relationship between board/administration and teachers, educational issues, and labor issues. Each team had prepared problems in question form on large sheets of paper, which were hung on the walls of the room—twenty-four on the board side and sixty-nine on the teachers' side. The protocols called for discussion of each question until four seconds of silence ensued, which would represent the exhaustion of that given question and trigger the facilitator's directing the group discussion on the next question. One board question would be discussed by both sides until its exhaustion, then one teacher question, another board question, and so on, until all ninety-three questions were completed.

The four hours on Friday passed quickly, but only the first three questions were discussed to completion. The more than twelve hours on Saturday resulted in the discussion of the remaining ninety questions. Throughout the day, meals were catered in so that discussion could continue and the mood of the process would not be interrupted.

On Sunday, the teams met to sort the ninety-three questions according to four categories, which would form the basis of the four committees that would actually negotiate the contract. No negotiations occurred that first weekend—only questioning and open discussion of issues, concerns, complaints, and hopes for the future. Also on Sunday the four committees were formed—Compensation and Benefits, Rights, Working Conditions, and Noncontractual Matters. On each committee, two board members and one resource person, that is, one of the three administrators, were assigned by the board president and two corresponding "voting members" and one of their resource persons were assigned by the association president. Each six-person committee then met, independently of the others, during the following three weeks in order to deal with the questions, or topics, of that committee as they had been assigned from the original ninety-three questions. During these three weeks, the board held meetings while the association members met in order to check with their respective colleagues on the directions of the committee sessions. The four committees thereby made commitments on behalf of their respective constituencies.

At the end of the three weeks of committee meetings—each committee met from four to six times—another prearranged weekend was organized for the resolution of unresolved issues. Again, all twenty participants met with the neutral facilitator in a sixteen-hour session on Saturday—the fourth weekend in June—until all issues were resolved and a contract was achieved. The commitment to meet until contract resolution was ever apparent during the process on that Saturday. Discussion was lively and sometimes emotionally charged, but it was always controlled; both the group process and the facilitator served as a guide to rationality and a positive focus. At any time, either side could call for a private meeting—an alternative to the traditional caucus—during this last marathon session.

When the contract was resolved at midnight, there were open expressions of elation shared among the board, administrators, and teacher representatives. On Monday, a committee of two board members, the assistant superintendent, the board attorney, and four teacher representatives met to write the final language on the contract. On Tuesday evening, the teachers' association met with the membership for ratification; on Wednesday evening, the board held a special meeting to ratify the contract. A party was held after that board meeting for all twenty participants. The process had formally begun on June 1, and both the ratification and celebration party occurred on June 27. District 230 had a new contract and, as had been predicted by Goldaber, both sides acknowledged that indeed both sides had won. Perhaps of more importance, the process had led to mutual trust in that several issues were settled by verbal agreement rather than by contract language.

Although not a panacea perhaps, win–win for District 230 brought about a mutually acceptable agreement; a greater level of understanding, trust, and respect; and a genuine board–association contract. The process included significantly nontraditional negotiations values; dramatically changed roles of administrators, board members, and attorney; an intensive time commitment; a prearranged time frame and commitment to cooperation; a new jargon born of the model; and, during the weekend sessions, the use of a neutral facilitator, whose role paradoxically was most effective because he controlled the process but sometimes did not speak for hours at a time.

In the win–win model, "there are no secrets" and the oneness can raise anxiety and a fear of vulnerability on both sides. However, in District 230, the mutual commitment to the process prevailed and resulted in the successful resolution of a two-year teachers' contract and an improved relationship between the board/administration and the teachers—and within thirty days.

RESEARCH ON WIN–WIN BARGAINING

Chapter 4 discussed some of the results of a 1999 national study of collective bargaining made by the author of this book. Several questions on win–win bargaining were included in this study. When the superintendents who were surveyed were asked if they had any experience with win–win bargaining (or with a similar concept under another name), 75.2 percent stated that they had participated in this type of bargaining. Since this concept is newer than that of traditional bargaining, this high response rate was somewhat surprising. Of course, this does not mean that 75 percent of the superintendents use this type of bargaining all the time. It does mean that three-quarters of them had used it at one time or another in their careers, perhaps, to try some new way to complete negotiations in a more positive way.

When the superintendents were asked if they thought that win–win was preferable to traditional adversarial bargaining, 61 percent stated that it was a better way to negotiate. Since only 9.9 percent indicated that it was not better, a significant number of superintendents did not have an opinion on this question.

One of the desired outcomes of win–win bargaining is a more positive and cooperative attitude between the teachers and the board/

administration. The superintendents were asked if this positive outcome was accomplished. Of those who responded, 60.3 percent said that the resulting attitude was more positive, with 13.5 percent stating that it was not more positive.

One criticism of win–win bargaining is that school districts may have to give up more money in this type of bargaining to maintain this positive attitude. The superintendents did not agree, as 53.2 percent said that they did not feel that their boards gave away more money and/or language in the contract in order to have a successful win–win session, as compared with traditional bargaining. There were 20.6 percent who said that they did have to give more away to the teachers under win–win bargaining.

Finally, the superintendents were asked in the study if they would recommend win–win bargaining. As might be expected from the other results, 61.7 percent stated that they would recommend it, with 13.5 percent not recommending win–win over traditional bargaining.[43]

NOTES

1. Chuck Namit and L. Swift, "Prescription for Labor Pains: Combine Bargaining with Problem-Solving," *American School Board Journal* 174 (July 1987): 24.

2. H. L. Schachter, "Win–Win Bargaining: A New Spirit in School Negotiations?" *Journal of Collective Negotiations* 18, no. 1 (1989): 1–8.

3. S. M. Johnson, "Can Schools Be Reformed at the Bargaining Table?" *Teachers College Record* 89 (1987): 269–79.

4. Karen M. Moriarty, "Thirty Days to a Contract" (paper presented to the Association of Negotiators and Contract Administrators, Clearwater Beach, Florida, November 7–9, 1984).

5. Gene Geisert, "The New Union Juggernaut Is Disguised as a Bandwagon," *Executive Educator* 8 (1989): 14–17.

6. Johnson, "Can Schools Be Reformed?" 269–79.

7. Moriarty, "Thirty Days." This article forms the second part of this chapter.

8. R. A. Hansen, "Good-Bye Adversarial Negotiations—We've Found a Better Way," *American School Board Journal* 176, no. 8 (1989): 23–24.

9. M. Cox and R. Stevens, "Here's Why We No Longer Dread Contract Negotiations," *American School Board Journal* 175, no. 2 (1988): 26, 41.

10. K. Jamieson and S. Jurist, "A Power Sharing Alternative," *Thrust* 10 (1988): 15–17.

11. Joni Lucas, "Decentralization: Key to New Boston Teacher Pact," *Education USA* 31, no. 6 (1989): 5.

12. Namit and Swift, "Prescription," 24.

13. Louis Peck, "Today's Teacher Unions Are Looking Well Beyond Collective Bargaining," *American School Board Journal* 175, no. 8 (1988): 32–36.

14. Iris McGinnis, "Boards Should Avoid the Bargaining Table," *American School Board Journal* 176, no. 8 (1989): 22–23.

15. Myron Lieberman, "Professional Ethics in Public Education: An Autopsy," *Kappan* 70 (1988): 159–60.

16. M. Pennella and S. Philips, "Help Your Board Negotiate: Stay Off the Bargaining Team," *Executive Educator* 9, no. 4 (1987): 28–29.

17. Chuck Namit, "The Union Has a Communication Strategy—and Your Board Should Too," *American School Board Journal* 173, no. 11 (1986): 30–31.

18. William Abel, "Collective Bargaining," *American Schools and Universities* 61 (February 1989): 43–44.

19. Moriarty, "Thirty Days."

20. Namit and Swift, "Prescription," 24.

21. Geisert, "New Union Juggernaut," 14–17.

22. J. W. Adair, "Informal Negotiations: 'Friendly' and Loosely Structured," *American School Board Journal* 168, no. 5 (1981): 38–39.

23. J. R. Huber and J. Hennies, "Fix on These Guiding Lights, and Emerge from the Bargaining Fog," *American School Board Journal* 174, no. 3 (1987): 31.

24. Schachter, "Win–Win Bargaining."

25. Schachter, "Win–Win Bargaining."

26. Thomas Bishop, "Collective Bargaining: Moving Away from the Battle," *Thrust* 10 (1988), 7–9.

27. Myron Lieberman, "Beware These Four Common Fallacies of School System Labor Relations," *American School Board Journal* 171, no. 6 (1984): 33.

28. Lieberman, "Professional Ethics," 1988, 159–60.

29. Abel, "Collective Bargaining," 43–44.

30. R. C. Kearney, *Labor Relations in the Public Sector* (New York: Dekker, 2001), 2.

31. John Glaser, "Alternative Labor Relations Practices: A Second Look," *Thrust* 18 (February–March 1989): 32–37.

32. Van Wilkinson, "Participatory Management vs. Participatory Responsibility," *Thrust* 10 (1988): 18–20.

33. Geisert, "New Union Juggernaut," 14–17.

34. J. B. Shedd, "Collective Bargaining, School Reform, and the Management of School Systems," *Educational Administration Quarterly* 24 (1988): 405–15.

35. Kearney, *Labor Relations,* 345.

36. Marilee Rist, "Here's What Empowerment Will Mean for Your Schools," *Executive Educator* 8 (1989): 16–19, 29.

37. Edward E. Eiler, "Follow These Golden Rules and Negotiate a Solid Labor Contract," *American School Board Journal* 176, no. 8 (1989): 25–26.

38. Moriarty, "Thirty Days," and Hansen, "Good-by," 23–24.

39. Kearney, *Labor Relations.*

40. Kearney, *Labor Relations,* 339.

41. Lucas, "Decentralization," 5.

42. B. O. Taylor and D. U. Levine, "Effective Schools Projects and School Based Management," *Kappan* 72, no. 1 (1991): 394–97.

43. William L. Sharp, "The Role of the Superintendent and School Board in Collective Bargaining: 1989–1999" (paper presented at the annual meeting of the Mid-Western Educational Research Association, Chicago, October 14, 1999).

9

STRIKES

Chapter 1 detailed the history of collective bargaining, including the beginning of teacher strikes in the public schools. This chapter discusses strikes in the public and private sectors, presents some recent research on school strikes, and gives specific suggestions for preparing for strikes in schools.

PUBLIC- VS. PRIVATE-SECTOR STRIKES

The word "strike" seems to come from the act of sailors hauling down their sails (which is called "striking" them) to quit work[1]; the Taft–Hartley Act (section 501 Id) defines a strike as "any concerted stoppage of work by employees . . . and any concerted slow-down or other concerted interruption of operations by employees." An example of another type of concerted slow-down is the "sick-in," a concerted action in which employees call in sick; this tactic is called the "blue flu" when it is used by the police and the "red rash" when it is used by firefighters.[2]

There are several differences between strikes in business and industry and strikes in the public sector. In the private sector, the employer manufactures a product (or sells a service) and there is usually a competing, alternate source for that product or service. If Ford goes on strike, it does not mean that an individual cannot purchase a car or get one serviced. Many other cars are available as are service providers.

The public sector, by contrast, usually provides a service for which there is no competing, alternate source. If the schools go on strike, parents do not have a realistic alternative. A parent could move to the next school district or enroll the children in a private school (if one is available), but these are not viable alternatives for most parents.

Another difference between public- and private-sector strikes is the type of pressure that is applied. In the private sector, economic pressure is present when the public cannot purchase the company's product. As a result, sales, profits, and possibly shareholder dividends are reduced. The pressure is on the company's management to stop the strike so that the product can be manufactured and sold. While the families of striking employees are very concerned about the strike, the general public does not cry out for a quick settlement. When Ford workers strike, very few people will raise a voice in protest.

In the public sector, the pressure is political in nature rather than economic. The school system that is on strike may not lose any revenue, or the revenue lost may be offset by the teachers' wages, which are not being paid. The pressure comes from the parents who have lost their only viable source of an education for their children. They put political pressure on the board members and administrators to settle the strike quickly and "get the kids back in school." They are not concerned with the principles or language issues involved in the collective bargaining process, and they are not very concerned with the salary issues. They are interested in the loss of services they have grown to expect.

Kearney notes that a lower percentage of employees in the public sector goes on strike than in the private sector and that public employees go on strike for a shorter period of time. He explains this difference by saying that government (public-sector) services are more essential, that public employees lack strike funds set up by the private-sector unions, and that there is political pressure and publicity for public unions to settle. And we should keep in mind that the private sector has actually shown a significant decline in strikes over the 1980s and 1990s as compared with the 1970s.[3]

RESEARCH ON STRIKES

An earlier chapter detailed some of the results from a 1999 national study on superintendents and collective bargaining researched by this author. Some of the questions in the study dealt with school strikes.

Despite the strikes we may hear and read about in the media, 75.2 percent of the school superintendents who responded in this survey stated that their present school district had never had a strike. Also, 92.2 percent of these superintendents had never been a superintendent during a strike.

While there may be the feeling that large, urban school districts have strikes and small districts do not, the research did not confirm this. There was no significant relationship between the size of the school district and whether it had had a strike.

There was a significant relationship between districts that went on strike and those that had a school attorney on the negotiating team. Keep in mind, however, that a causal relationship cannot be assumed from these data. It could be that districts that anticipate strikes tended to want attorneys on the negotiating team to represent them.

There was no significant relationship between strikes and board members on the negotiating team who lacked negotiating expertise. However—and this is important—there was a significant relationship between strikes and the teacher organization's bypassing the board's negotiating team and going directly to the board. And, as the districts increased in size, the extent to which the teacher organizations bypassed the negotiating teams increased. An implication may be that boards, especially in larger districts, should try to avoid letting the teacher organizations bypass their team and go directly to the full board.[4]

STATE RESPONSES TO STRIKES

One of the reasons that states have established mandatory collective bargaining laws is that some districts were negotiating (or trying to negotiate) and going on strike, often illegally. Despite no-strike clauses in contracts, court orders, restraining orders, injunctions, and the jailing of striking teachers, strikes still occurred.

Another reason that states passed mandatory collective bargaining laws was the hope that fewer strikes would occur in the future. Strikes did decline in states such as Ohio, Illinois, and Minnesota, which passed mandatory collective bargaining laws that permitted strikes.[5] To use Ohio as an example, the 2001 annual report of the State Employment Relations Board listed the number of strikes before passage of the mandatory collective bargaining law in 1984:

1978 – 67 strikes
1979 – 56 strikes
1980 – 60 strikes
1981–1983 – no data available

Next are the numbers of strikes after the law was passed in 1984:

1984 – 4 strikes
1985 – 9 strikes
1987 – 19 strikes (the largest since 1984)
1999 – 6 strikes
2000 – 2 strikes
2001 – 8 strikes (6 in education)[6]

State legislatures also began to establish procedures to deal with collective bargaining that they hoped would reduce the number of strikes in their states:

- mediation bureaus were established to help resolve disputes;
- fact finders were called in to schools to gather data from both sides and report their findings; and
- arbitrators were hired to judge between the two sides on various issues.

While each of these procedures has been effective for some schools, other school districts managed to progress through all these procedures and have a strike. Thus, school officials need to be aware of the possibility of a teacher strike and need to be prepared for it.

PREPARATION FOR A STRIKE

This next section briefly mentions some general procedures in preparing for a strike; it is followed by a section listing procedures for districts that decide to keep schools open and a section listing procedures for those that choose to close the schools.

General Procedures

General procedures for school districts preparing for a strike, whether schools remain open or closed, are:

1. Establish communication links. The regular telephone services may be jammed by community callers or by the union. The administration and the board need to be able to communicate easily and quickly. Private, unlisted lines with telephone numbers known by a limited number of people can be installed and used throughout the year. Also, many districts purchase laptop computers for their board members and establish e-mail accounts for them. These can be used for communication if everyone knows to check their mail on a regular basis.

2. Get public relations help. If the district has a public relations person on staff, that person should do some research prior to the strike: for example, contact other schools that have had strikes and see what successes and failures they have had concerning public relations in the community. If the district has no public relations person, it might want to employ a professional public relations firm on a short-term basis to advise the district on dealing with the media, the parents and community, and the staff.

3. Be prepared for mailings. Run off a couple of sets of address labels for the parents and the staff. Establish procedures for getting a group of secretaries together quickly to duplicate, stuff, and mail letters.

4. Designate a spokesperson. The board of education should agree on one spokesperson in case of a strike: the superintendent, an assistant superintendent, the board president, or the chief negotiator. Since most inquiries will be made to the school district office, it is usually best for the spokesperson to be an employee rather than a board member or outside negotiator, as the latter individuals may not be readily available.

The board and the spokesperson should make everyone aware that only this one person speaks for the board and administration during the strike.

5. Do not agree to a news blackout. As stated in an earlier chapter, both sides usually agree to a news blackout during negotiations—and they often follow it faithfully. However, it is different during a strike. Remember that the teachers need to apply public political pressure against the board. And while the actual issues are not vital to the public, the teachers will feel the need to demonstrate that their position is a reasonable one. So, blackout or no blackout, the union will tell its side to the community. The board has to retain its right to express its views as well, demonstrating its openness rather than stating that it refuses to discuss any issues.

6. Prepare an emergency resolution. The board of education should pass a resolution granting emergency authority to the superintendent, in the event of a strike, for the duration of the strike. This shows confidence in the administration and allows the superintendent to take any reasonable action necessary to aid the school district. The board cannot be expected to be available to meet formally to make every decision necessary during the strike. Obviously, the superintendent has to keep in contact with the board by phone or e-mail and keep them informed about all the decisions he or she makes.

7. Develop an athletic policy. Some athletic conferences have a strike policy that will cover all conference games during a strike. However, the policy probably will not cover games with nonconference schools, and policies for practice sessions will probably not be mentioned. The administration should discuss this and make a recommendation to the board. Part of the decision will be based on whether the board has decided to close the schools or remain open during the strike. If the schools are closed by a strike, then there should be no athletics— practice or contests. School equipment should be locked up and not issued to coaches (who may want to practice off campus). If the schools remain open, the decision may depend on whether coaches strike, on whether trainers are available, and on safety considerations.

Procedures for an Open School

All the procedures mentioned previously should be discussed prior to a strike, and they should be discussed regardless of whether the schools will remain open or be closed during the strike. The next group of procedures described are designed to help the district prepare if it decides to remain open during a teacher strike.

1. Get substitute lists. Most school districts have a list of substitute teachers. These lists should be obtained from nearby districts prior to any strike and examined for duplications and for the qualifications of the people listed. If time permits, the school district should write or call these people to see if they would be interested in substituting in the event of a strike. If the strike appears to be inevitable, it would be worthwhile to invite substitutes to the district for individual conferences in order to make copies of their teaching certificates and determine their qualifications and experiences. This could be done on a weekend with several administrators available to talk to the potential substitutes.

2. Increase substitute pay. Schools must pay substitutes more during a strike because of the potential harassment and working conditions. The board of education (or the superintendent under emergency authority) should approve a special substitute pay and prepare advertisements for the newspapers. (Some states require special wording for substitute ads during a strike.)

3. Arrange for transportation. Substitutes and students need to feel safe when coming to the school buildings. Work out details on security, routes, parking lots, and possible shuttle services for substitutes parking in secure lots.

4. Determine whether other staff members will strike. If the teachers strike, will others follow? If the district employs bus drivers, will they continue to drive? Will the secretaries, cafeteria personnel, and custodians come to school? This situation varies a great deal from district to district and does not depend solely on whether the other staffs are unionized. If the administration finds that everyone will go on strike to support the teachers, it should consider closing the schools.

5. Meet and communicate. The superintendent should meet with the administrative staff on a continuing basis and discuss all the items mentioned in this chapter, seeking the input and advice from the administrative team. Also, the team should make plans to meet daily during the strike to discuss what happened that day and what should be done for the next day. A time and place should be established for a meeting at the end of the first strike day. A principal may feel very much alone in his or her building all day during a strike and needs to know that there is a private line to the superintendent's office, as well as a scheduled meeting that afternoon with the superintendent and other administrators.

6. Arrange for security. The local police department should be contacted prior to the strike to alert it to possible problems involving security, traffic, and vandalism. Some departments are more cooperative than others during a strike since police are also public employees. It may be necessary to hire private security forces to watch over school buildings at night. (And it may be necessary to include school officials' properties and businesses in police patrols.)

7. Notify the attorney. If the school attorney is not involved in the negotiations process, he or she should be notified that a strike is possible and that the school will remain open. The school administration should be able to contact the school attorney on short notice, day and night, for advice. Find out when, where, and how the attorney can be contacted.

8. Develop an appropriate curriculum. It may be necessary to modify the current curriculum for some classes to make it appropriate for the substitutes who will be teaching. For example, at the elementary level, it might be advisable to concentrate on a few subjects during the day instead of trying to teach everything that is usually scheduled. If the strike lasts more than a few days, the curriculum can be expanded. At the high school level, substitutes may not be qualified to teach, for example, physics, calculus, and German. In this case, the school may have to hold some generic courses in mathematics and science. Obviously, it would be ideal to have a group of substitute teachers who can teach every course in the curriculum. Realistically, the school will probably have substitutes who can better handle freshman regular classes than senior honors classes. The point is that the administration needs to interview the potential substitutes (as described earlier) and decide what curriculum can be offered to the students during the strike.

9. Decide who comes to school. While some administrators can plan ahead adequately and know that they can handle all the students who will show up during a strike, others may not be able to do the same thing. In some cases, the district needs to open one school, or one grade level, at a time as substitutes are hired. This gives the district time to work on the substitute/curriculum situation gradually. For example, if the high school has enough substitute teachers to staff only the freshman curriculum, it does not make sense to bring in all students. As the number of substitutes increases, additional grade levels can be returned to the school.

Procedures for a Closed School

Obviously, if the board decides to close the schools during a strike, the task of the administration is much easier. Next are recommended procedures for districts electing to close the schools.

1. Protect the workers. If only the teachers go on strike, many other staff members will be crossing picket lines, parking their cars, and walking into the buildings. While the harassment of these employees can range from intense to nonexistent, depending on the district and its history, the administration must be prepared. Look to the past: What has happened in the past is a good indication of what could happen during this strike. Make sure that all employees feel secure and know where to park, what to expect, and what to say (or not to say).

2. Keep regular hours. Do not dismiss employees early. Leaving early gives the strikers one more argument against the district.

3. Keep "crossing" teachers busy. If some teachers choose to ignore the strike and report to work, they have the right to do so. They should be kept busy working on something educational. Instead of telling them to read the newspaper or watch television, they should asked to earn their pay by working on curriculum projects, doing some library or laboratory research, or accomplishing something else that is constructive and educational. One school district organized a series of field trips for its teachers, taking them to museums, science laboratories, biological field sites, libraries, and courts. The teachers had to cross the picket lines on the first day to indicate their decisions on the strike. However, after that day, they were told to report to an alternate location (a library in town), where they left for the daily field trip that had been arranged by the administration.

Should the Schools Stay Open?

There are both "yes" and "no" answers to the question of whether to keep the schools open.

YES. Keeping the schools open and functioning sends out a message to the striking teachers: Education is still going on and teachers are losing pay. This puts economic pressure on the teachers who are on strike. While laws differ in the various states, some states require that any missed days of school be made up at full salary pay. (For other states, this may be negotiable.) Thus, if the district is functioning, the days do not need to be made up.

NO. Keeping the schools closed lessens the hard feelings that inevitably accompany a strike. No confrontation occurs between striking teachers and substitutes, and between strikers and students trying to attend schools. If the administration cannot hire an adequate number of substitute teachers, it should not open the school. Likewise, if it feels it cannot maintain a safe environment for staff and students, it is wise not to open the schools.

PROCEDURES DURING A STRIKE

Once a strike has begun, standard procedures should be followed:

1. Be ready for calls. Prepare written responses to the typical questions that will be asked:

How many students are there in school?
What is going on?
Is the school safe?
Are the subs qualified?
Is lunch being served?
Why is the school open? Closed?
Is evening school (or a ball game, a concert) cancelled?

The secretaries can field many of these inquiries and provide consistent answers, referring more complex questions to the designated spokesperson. As new questions come in, the "question–answer sheet" can be revised.

2. Meet with administrators. As stated earlier, it is essential to hold daily debriefing sessions with the administrative staff to keep them informed and to allow them to ask questions.

3. State facts. When answering questions, especially from the press, state facts. Do not react to union statements, except to correct inaccurate information.

4. Warn the board and staff. Inform the board members, administrators, and staff members that they may receive harassing phone calls or letters, or may be confronted by picketers at work or at home. The school attorney should instruct the board on what is legal and what is not legal, with regard to strike activities.

5. Prepare for board meetings. The board and the administration should make additional preparations for any board meeting held during a strike:

- Attendance can swell from the usual six or eight to several hundred. Have adequate seating or even schedule the meeting for a gym or auditorium.
- Make sure the board members and administrative personnel have reserved parking with adequate supervision.
- Have appropriate, visible security in the parking lots and in the meeting room.
- Have a workable public-address system, with microphones available at the board table and for the audience.
- Be prepared to have union members handing out strike information, including "fact sheets" and position papers. Consider preparing similar documents giving the board's position.
- Review the agenda. Is it necessary to cover all the items planned for this meeting or can some be postponed? Remember that the crowd is coming to discuss the strike, not to hear a debate on remedial reading or the remodeling of the middle school. Are there any agenda items that could be embarrassing: administrative salary raises, the announcement of additional state funds, grievances?
- At the beginning of the board meeting, have the board president explain the board's agenda and procedures for the evening: "We have two or three legal necessities that we must approve tonight—like paying our monthly bills—and then we will get to the issue for which you came tonight. We will move through these first items very quickly and not keep you waiting."
- Have a strategy worked out for hearing from the public, the teachers, and the board members. Do not let any one person or group

dominate the evening. Allow all views to be expressed. Do not allow the public to insist on a polling of the board on issues that are still being negotiated.

- Retain control of the meeting.
- Be sure to follow the state's laws on public and executive (closed) board meetings, special meetings, and prior notifications to the public and the press.

In addition to these specific procedures, it is important to realize in general that the old Boy Scout motto, "Be prepared," is really important in a strike situation. The well-prepared administrator maintains files for crisis situations such as closing a school due to weather, a tragedy in the school, and school strikes. Whenever the administrator sees a good journal article on strike preparation, reads some newspaper article on a nearby district's strike, or reads some research that may be helpful, he or she should put it into the "strike procedures" file. For example, this author has the following (among other items) in his strike procedures file:

- a newspaper ad for substitute teachers during a strike in a neighboring school district;
- a national research service's report on planning for strikes;
- possible activities planned for nonstriking teachers if the schools are closed;
- notes on administrative planning meetings during previous strikes;
- memos from other superintendents to their administrators regarding planning for a strike;
- the athletic conference's policy statement on games during a strike (part of the policy is that if a contest is cancelled due to a strike, the striking school receives a defeat and the contest is not rescheduled); and
- letters to parents during a strike (examples from several districts).

The school board and the administration should always keep this in mind during a strike: The strike will eventually end and school will resume. What each side says and does may be long remembered. Personal behavior, the wording of letters and press notices, and public pronouncements may be remembered for years. While school officials should take a strong stance in defending their official positions, they also should be very careful about the words they use and the actions they take in that defense.

Inevitably, some bad feelings result from a strike. Part of the next chapter gives some suggestions for dealing with the aftermath of a strike.

SUMMARY

This chapter discussed the differences between public- and private-sector strikes, discussed some research on strikes, and told how states had reacted to strikes. Next, the chapter listed some general procedures for dealing with strikes, and included suggestions for those schools that remain open during a strike and those that close. The next chapter discusses the management of the contract that has been negotiated.

DISCUSSION QUESTIONS

1. Discuss the purpose of a strike in the private sector versus one in the public sector.
2. Why is it important to have one spokesperson during a strike?
3. How should the board deal with the media during a strike?
4. Discuss the importance of communications during a strike.
5. What are the advantages and disadvantages of keeping the schools open during a strike?
6. Discuss the preparation necessary for a board meeting during a strike.
7. How have states responded to strikes?
8. Discuss what can be done to prepare for a strike in terms of the following:

   –substitute teachers
   –transportation
   –security
   –the curriculum

NOTES

1. R. C. Kearney, *Labor Relations in the Public Sector* (New York: Dekker, 2001), 233.

2. Kearney, *Labor Relations,* 223.

3. Kearney, *Labor Relations,* 224–25.

4. William L. Sharp, "The Role of the Superintendent and School Board in Collective Bargaining: 1989–1999" (paper presented at the annual meeting of the Mid-Western Educational Research Association, Chicago, October 14, 1999), 7, 21, 25.

5. Kearney, *Labor Relations,* 239.

6. SERB Annual Report 2001 (Columbus: Ohio State Employment Relations Board, 2001), 14.

10

CONTRACT MANAGEMENT

This chapter makes suggestions for dealing with the negative feelings that result from a strike and tells how to educate the administrative staff on the new contract. One part of contract management is the handling of grievances concerning the contract. This chapter examines this area in detail.

HEALING THE WOUNDS

When negotiations are finally completed, the important job of contract management begins. If the negotiations were typical of those at many schools, the relationship between the teachers and the board/administration may not be as good as either would like. So the first thing to do is to try improving this relationship. Some ideas that have worked in the past are presented next.

Hold a joint press conference to announce the end of negotiations and describe the resulting contract. If this is done, both sides should have input in the press release and know what the press has been told. If only one side gives the information, it is likely to be somewhat biased. If the district has a public relations person, that individual can help in arranging the press conference and the formal statement.

Although it may be tough to do, the wise administrator will recognize the union negotiators publicly at the next faculty meeting and state what a good job they did in representing the teachers.

Depending on the severity of the feelings at the conclusion of negotiations, a district may want to establish a labor–management committee, patterned after those of the private sector, to meet on a regular basis to discuss mutual concerns. This committee forum does not take the place of the grievance procedure, but it probably will reduce the number of grievances since some topics can be discussed before they reach the point in which a grievance is filed. Similarly, the committee should not be a negotiating committee. That is over for now. People on the committee representing both the teachers and the administration should not be expected to sit through more meetings just to hear the old negotiations proposals. The purpose of the committee is to provide a forum for discussion and, occasionally, a solution to problems.

The superintendent or some top official should meet on a regular basis with the union president or the union officials. This serves a similar function as the committee just described, but is less formal. Also, if only two or three people are involved, some of the posturing that occurs in committees should be eliminated. This writer met with the union president for lunch once a month (alternating on who should pay) to hear concerns and answer questions.

Another possibility to improve the relationship is to have the superintendent (or designee) and some board members go to each school and meet with the faculty (on a voluntary basis). Again, the purpose is to provide a forum for discussion. If this is done, the administration/board group must be careful in answering (or avoiding) questions that are relevant only to that particular school building. They probably do not have enough information to answer all such questions, but it is good to hear the questions. It tells the visiting group something about the feelings and concerns in that building.

It is probably best to try a variety of techniques to show that the board and administration want to make the effort to improve relations with the staff. Despite of any negative feelings the teachers may have, they cannot ignore the fact that the board is making the effort to improve the situation.

EDUCATING THE ADMINISTRATIVE STAFF

Another task is educating the administrative staff on the new contract. As soon as possible, make copies of the new contract (or at least the changes to the old contract), even if it means copying handwritten or poorly typed pages. The important thing is getting accurate information quickly into the hands of the administrative staff. (It is very useful to have the entire contract on a computer disk, and update it as new contract sections are negotiated. This makes it is easy to generate copies of the new contract.)

The chief negotiator or spokesman for the board team should meet with the administrative staff, hand out the contract, and explain all the changes, giving emphasis to areas affecting those present. He should explain why the changes were made, what the complaints were that led to the teacher proposals in the first place, and what emotions seem to be involved in certain issues discussed during negotiations. These administrators are the people who will manage the contract; they need to have this information in order to manage it well.

If a school district's size allows, it is best to have all the administrative staff at the same meeting instead of holding different meetings for each building or area. The principals need to be aware that they have to interpret and enforce the contract the same way in each school.

With any new contract, there will be questions even after this orientation session. Administrators should be told to contact a central-office person who is familiar with the new contract (and, if possible, one who participated on the team). In this way, there can be consistency in the answers given throughout the district.

Finally, the administrators in the district should be reminded that the administration (board) retains all rights not restricted by inclusion in the contract. Teachers have been known to state, "You can't do that; it isn't in the contract."

RESPONDING TO GRIEVANCES

Grievances are usually filed at step one, the building level. When the principal receives a grievance, the central-office person who has been designated to handle grievances should be contacted. Since grievances are sometimes filed in different buildings on the same topic, it is important that the administrative response be consistent throughout the district. The central-office administrator can advise the principal of other, similar grievances, past or present, and discuss appropriate responses.

In most grievance procedures, the teacher filing the grievance meets with the principal to discuss the grievance. At this meeting, it is appropriate for the principal to listen, question, take notes, and tell the teacher that he or she will respond in writing by the contract deadline (or before). At this point, the principal should contact the central office, if this has not previously been done, as described previously.

The principal (with appropriate guidance) must decide whether the contract has been violated and how to answer the grievance, as well as consider the remedy sought. It is possible that the contract was violated but that the remedy, in the opinion of the administration, is too much, in spite of the violation.

When the principal answers the grievance, a copy of the grievance and the response is sent to the central office; another copy is kept in the principal's office.

The teacher and union then have to decide whether to pursue further steps. In many schools, the next step is to take the grievance to the central office, with further steps involving the superintendent (if he is not involved at the previous step), the school board (see the opinion in the section on grievance procedures and the board step in chapter 5), and possibly, some kind of arbitration.

Figure 10.1 is an example of a grievance and of a superintendent's response to that grievance.

Notice the superintendent's response to Sue Smith. In the first paragraph, he gives, for the record, the date that the grievance was originally filed, the date that it was filed in the superintendent's office, the date on which he and Ms. Smith met to discuss it, and the fact that she had a representative with her. (By the way, "date filed" means the date the grievance was received by the administrator, not the day it was typed or sent by the grievant.)

The next paragraph states the grievant's situation as stated by her, without editorial comment by the superintendent. The paragraph after that summarizes the remedy she seeks.

EXAMPLE OF A GRIEVANCE (FROM SMITH)

To: Superintendent
From: Sue Smith
Date: November 10, _____
Re: Level II Grievance

During the week of August 27, _____, I served on jury duty at the _____ Court. A copy of the certificate which was supplied to me was sent earlier.

According to the Agreement, faculty members are paid for the time they are serving on jury duty.

XV Salary Procedures

3. The Board shall pay the regular salary to staff members called to serve as jurors, but there shall be deducted therefrom the amount received by the teacher for such jury duty, except those moneys paid to the teacher by the courts for transportation and parking.

Upon return to school I was told that I should turn in my verification of jury duty and that I would be paid for that time. After waiting for three pay periods, I was not paid, nor did I receive any response concerning this matter from the school district office. I inquired about the status of this problem on October 19 to the secretary. She had originally sent my form to the administrative center. I was referred to the principal.

On October 23, I met with the principal and was told that I was not going to be paid for that time. On October 29, I telephoned the district office to determine exactly where that decision was made. I was directed to the Personnel Director, who told me that he had made the decision.

I am requesting payment for the time I was on jury duty as provided for in the Agreement.

cc: Principal
       Chairman, Welfare Committee

EXAMPLE OF A RESPONSE TO A GRIEVANCE (TO SMITH)

To: Ms. Sue Smith
From: Superintendent
Date: November 17, _____
Re: Grievance

This is the administrative response at Level Two of your grievance filed with Principal _____ on November 3, _____ and with me on November 12, _____. We met to discuss this grievance on November 15, _____, along with your association representative.

You have stated that you served on jury duty from August 27–31, _____ (5 days). According to Article XV, Section 3, teachers called to serve on jury duty should receive their regular salary. You were not paid for these days.

continued

Figure 10.1. Example of Grievance (from Smith) and Response

You have asked, as a remedy, to be paid for the five days of jury duty.

The purpose of Article XV, Section 3, is to make sure that teachers do not suffer a loss of pay for serving on jury duty, a civic responsibility. The assumption, of course, is that school is in session and that a teacher on jury duty is missing a day of work. Certainly, no teacher is paid a regular salary when jury duty is during a vacation or holiday season or during the summer. Or, it could be argued that, during these times, the "regular salary" is "no pay" and this is continued.

During August 27–31, _____ school was not in session due to a teachers' strike. Had you reported to work, you would have received a "regular salary." Had you decided to take part in the strike, you would not have been paid for these days. If the strike lasted from August 27–31, exclusively, we would have had an interesting question: Would you have reported to work (and been paid) if there had been no jury duty? While both sides could have argued the merits of "yes" or "no," no real evidence could have been brought to bear on this issue.

However, the strike lasted until the morning of September 14, _____, a total of thirteen strike days. From September 4 through September 13, a period of eight weekdays, you could have reported to work or participated in the strike. Your decision was to participate in the strike for the entire eight days. Thus, we feel we have adequate evidence that, given a choice in the first week, you would have chosen a similar avenue. We have no evidence to suggest that, absent the jury duty, you would have reported to work for five days (August 27–31) and then taken part in the strike for eight days.

It is my opinion that Article XV, Section 3, has not been violated. The intent of the language—to prevent teachers from losing regular pay for a civic responsibility—has been preserved. To pay a striking teacher for serving on jury duty would be a perversion of this language. As a result, I must respectfully deny your grievance and the remedy which you have sought.

cc: Principal
      Association President

Figure 10.1.   *continued*

The next three paragraphs explain the superintendent's opinion of the situation and his interpretation of the contract. The final paragraph offers the superintendent's decision on the grievance.

While administrative responses to grievances do not have to follow this pattern, it is best to include the information shown in this example (a real one, by the way).

Look at the Tim Brown grievance and the response to it in figure 10.2.

In the section on bargaining strategies in chapter 5, it was mentioned that grievances should state the exact article and section that have been violated. This grievance is a good example of one that did not do this. As a result, the superintendent felt he could not answer it. Administrators receiving a grievance like this one should not guess what the violation is supposed to be or what article is supposed to have been violated. The

EXAMPLE OF A GRIEVANCE (FROM BROWN)

To: Superintendent
From: Tim Brown, Association President
Re: Grievance
Date: June 26, _____

Your memo of June 18, _____ constitutes, on the part of the Board, a refusal to bargain the terms, conditions, and compensation for the Director of Activities at _____ H.S. and the Computer Lab Supervisor at each high school.

The Agreement has been violated in the following articles:

Article I
Article III
Article V
Article VII
Article XXIII
Article XXV
Article XXVI
Article XXVIII

The remedy in this matter is the prompt resumption of bargaining for the Director of Activities and Computer Lab Supervisor and the rescission of your actions to unilaterally implement these positions without consent of the Association.

cc: UniServ Director

EXAMPLE OF A RESPONSE TO A GRIEVANCE (TO BROWN)

To: Mr. Tim Brown
From: Superintendent
Date: July 12, _____
Re: Grievance

This is the administrative response at Level Two of your grievance filed with me on June 26, _____, and about which we met on July 5, _____.

You stated that the Board refused to bargain terms, conditions, and compensation for the Director of Activities at _____ H.S. and the Computer Lab Supervisors at each of the high schools. You stated that the following articles were violated: I, III, V, VII, XXIII, XXV, XXVI, XXVIII.

You asked, as a remedy, that the Board resume bargaining for the above positions and not implement these positions.

In writing answers to grievances for nine years, I have always tried to take each alleged violation and state the administration's position on it. However, when I looked up your list of 8 articles which had been violated, I found that there were 31 sections in these 8 articles. When I talked to you to define the actual violations, you merely read Article I to me,

continued

Figure 10.2. Example of a Grievance (from Brown) and a Response

then read Article III to me and said our actions did not "conform to the Agreement." You stated that we did not "operate within the confines of the description" of Article V. You gave a similar response to my inquiries about the other articles.

Let us look at the first two articles mentioned, Recognition and Board's Rights:

We have never recognized any other agent as the bargaining agent. How can the Association say we have done so? Also, how can the Board violate Article III, titled "Board's Rights?"

It seems obvious that the Association is "grasping at straws" to make a case. Certainly, I am not able to answer this grievance in the usual manner.

(The superintendent's response goes on to explain his view on what had happened but does not answer the grievance directly on any of the other articles mentioned. The Association later dropped the grievance and admitted that the Board did have the right to establish positions in the school system. The Board negotiated the salaries of these positions when negotiations began.)

Figure 10.2. *continued*

grievant should be very specific on the violation and the location in the contract pertaining to the violation.

The John S. Gone grievance (fig. 10.3) is given for the reader to answer, using the pattern established previously. Following the grievance is the contract page that applies to the grievance. The suggested response is listed at the end of this chapter (fig. 10.4).

To: Superintendent
From: John S. Gone
Re: Grievance, Level Two

On June 5, I had to leave school to meet a swimming pool repairman at my home. I did not miss any classes, as I left at about 9:05 and returned to school at about 9:45. My preparation period is from 9:00 to 9:55 a.m. My principal said he was going to place a disciplinary note in my file and might deduct pay in the future if I did this again. I did not miss any class time and went during my prep period like the contract says. I even signed out and signed back in again in the office.

Contract violation: VII-8, page 8.
Remedy: Take the letter out of my file!

Article VII-8 reads as follows:

Teachers shall be permitted to leave the building during a preparation period when necessary to perform tasks related to their teaching duties. Preparation periods are part of the normal school day and are necessary for good teaching. Prior to leaving, the teacher will initial the log. Upon return by the end of the period, the teacher will also initial the log. These conditions may be waived by the principal or his or her designee depending upon individual circumstances.

Figure 10.3.   Grievance Example for Reader

Here are some general guidelines on grievances:

- Try to settle at the lowest level, if possible.
- Look at the contract. Make sure the grievant states the specific article and section violated as well as how it was violated and when. Was this a violation? Was it filed in a timely manner?
- The designated central-office administrator should examine negotiations notes if the grievance involves a new section of the contract. Was this problem discussed during negotiations?
- If the administration is wrong and the contract is being violated, it is best to admit it quickly at the lowest possible level and settle the grievance.

GRIEVANCE ARBITRATION

In the event that a grievance goes all the way to arbitration, here are some suggestions for the arbitration hearing.

The arbitration hearing is like a small, informal trial, with an arbitrator as the "judge" and someone representing the union and someone for the board acting as "attorneys" for both sides (both often are attorneys as well).

Both sides are given a list of names of possible arbitrators weeks before any hearing. Each side gets to "strike" a name off the list until only one name is left. It is wise for the administrator to consult with the district's attorney, negotiator, or school board association to check into the biographical information on the possible arbitrators. Their backgrounds and previous decisions may suggest who should be eliminated from consideration.

Prior to the hearing, the administration and the person representing them at the hearing should review the contract, all the grievance steps and documents, past practices in the area of concern, and discussions and actions during negotiations on this topic; then, they should talk to any administrators involved in the situation that resulted in the filing of the grievance.

Kearney discusses a newer form of arbitration called expedited, or instant, arbitration. The purpose of this type of arbitration is to reach a conclusion sooner and at a reduced cost. The key is to select those grievances that are less complicated for use in this process. The arbitration hearing is less formal than the one described previously and does not resemble a trial as much as the traditional hearing. The arbitrator, in some cases, may declare the decision immediately and, in others, may do so in just a few days. There are some fears that because the procedure is cheaper and less formal, more grievances may be filed and that the arbitrators, in making quick decisions, may make poorer decisions in expedited arbitration.[1]

The Arbitration Hearing

If the administration has followed the suggestions that were stated in the previous section, they should be adequately prepared for the hearing. Below is a description of a typical hearing and suggestions for the conduct of the administration during the hearing.

- Be on time to the arbitration. Ask the arbitrator how the hearing room (probably a school conference room or a classroom) should be set up: Where should tables be placed? How many should there be? Should there be a witness table?
- As the arbitration begins, the arbitrator usually tells those present how the meeting will proceed. Listen and follow the procedures the arbitrator outlines.
- Usually, each side is told to give an opening statement explaining its position. The union, bringing the grievance, goes first.
- State the case clearly. Make sure the arbitrator understands the administration's position. But do not continually repeat the same point.
- The burden is on the union to prove that the administration violated the contract. It is a good idea to remind the arbitrator about this.
- Remember that this is not a real court with state laws and judicial tradition. The arbitrator may be quite liberal in what evidence and testimony is accepted—more liberal than a court judge would be. The arbitrator may state, "I will let you show me the evidence and then I will decide later whether it is admissible."

- Be courteous and do not object too often, especially if it is obvious that the arbitrator finds objections frustrating to the announced procedures.
- Do not call witnesses unless they are really needed and the administration knows what the witnesses will say.
- Often, at the conclusion, the arbitrator will ask whether both sides want to offer an oral summary or submit a brief (a written summary of both positions and why the position of the side offering the brief is the correct one). Unless the arbitrator offers a choice, do both.

Following the hearing, the arbitrator usually will take several weeks to study the testimony and evidence, read the briefs, reach a decision, and send a copy of the decision to both sides.

The administration should study the decision (and the instructions for a remedy if the contract was violated) and notify the appropriate administrative personnel of the decision. It may also be appropriate to consult with the district's attorney for advice.

To: Mr. John S. Gone
From: Superintendent
Re: Grievance
Date: (within limit)

    This is the administrative response at Level Two of your grievance filed with me on May 15, _____, and about which we met on May 19, _____.

    You have stated that the principal has placed a disciplinary note in your file because you left school during your preparation period to meet a swimming pool repairman at your home. You stated that Article VII, Section 8, had been violated by the principal's action.

    You asked, as a remedy, that the note be taken out of your file.

    Article VII, Section 8, permits a teacher to leave school during the preparation period to "perform tasks related to their teaching duties." You have stated that your purpose for leaving was to meet a swimming pool repairman at your home. Your trip was not at all related to your duties as an English teacher.

    It is my opinion that Article VII, Section 8, has not been violated. The permission in the Article to leave school does not extend to personal duties, only professional ones. As a result, I must respectfully deny your grievance and the remedy which you have sought.

Figure 10.4. Answer to Grievance Example

SUMMARY

This chapter gave some suggestions on how to "heal the wounds" from difficult negotiations or a strike. It then discussed the importance of educating the administrative staff about the contents of the new contract. It concluded with a discussion of grievances, how to respond to them, and how to approach the arbitration of grievances. The next chapter is a simulation activity, designed to give the readers of this book an opportunity to try out their skills at negotiations.

DISCUSSION QUESTIONS

1. Describe some efforts that could be made to "heal the wounds" following a strike.
2. Discuss the importance of informing all administrators about the new contract provisions.
3. What steps should a principal take when presented with a formal, written grievance?
4. Discuss how to prepare for a grievance arbitration hearing.
5. What are the usual arbitration hearing procedures?
6. Discuss the labor–management committee concept.
7. What advice would you give if it is discovered that the board did violate the contract?

NOTES

1. R. C. Kearney, *Labor Relations in the Public Sector* (New York: Dekker, 2001), 318–19.

11

NEGOTIATIONS SIMULATION

This chapter is intended to describe a simulation for providing experience in negotiations. This simulation exercise can be used by a university class or can be an in-service project for administrators. It has been used several times at the university graduate level (for collective bargaining courses) with much success. Students have commented that the experience was very helpful to them in understanding how bargaining actually works at the bargaining table. They felt they had the opportunity to learn why timing is important, how the wording of contract language proposals is crucial, and how to listen, react, and respond to the proposals from the other side.

PROCEDURES

The instructor (or group leader) should divide the group into teams representing the board of education and the teachers. It seems to work well with two or three people on a board team and the same number representing the teachers. For example, a group of twenty-four can be divided into four "tables," with three people negotiating for the board on one side and three for the teachers on the other side of each table. (Whether there is an actual table between them or just regular classroom desks does not seem to make any difference.) If this is done with a university class, it is wise to ask each student the extent of his or her prior bargaining experience and whether it occurred on a board team or on the teachers' team. The instructor can then assign the teams so that each has a similar amount of experience. (It is also interesting to place experienced teacher negotiators on a board team and vice versa. This gives the students a chance to argue the "other side" of an issue.) The instructor may want to modify the salary schedule that is listed in the exercise or add or delete an area of language to make the simulation more relevant locally. The simulation material, as presented, has been used with university classes for two consecutive class sessions of approximately one and one-half hours each. It can easily be expanded for additional sessions.

Once the teams are assigned, all participants should be given the following general instructions:

1. If the state has a mandatory bargaining law, the participants need to know whether or not to "follow the state law when you are negotiating." The instructor may want to include or exclude something from the law so that the simulation fits better into the law in the state.
2. The "negotiators" should read the information that follows these procedures. This information describes the city, the school district, and the district's budget as well as listing of the areas to be negotiated. The participants should read for significant facts they can use in their arguments to support their positions.
3. Each team (of two or three) should meet to discuss this material and prepare their "demands" (from the teachers) and some possible "responses" (from the board). While the board teams do not know exactly what the teachers will put in their proposals, they can decide what their position will be—how far they are willing to go on the issues. (Instructors or group leaders should note that this discussion and planning will require some time and should not take away from the time planned for the actual negotiation sessions.)
4. When both sides are prepared, they should sit across from each other in the manner usually found in negotiation sessions. The teacher team should begin by presenting its proposals to the board

team. (The room should be large enough for this to occur simultaneously in several groups.) As explained in an earlier chapter, the board team should listen to the teacher requests and ask clarifying questions during the first session.

5. Either side can "caucus" when it wants to discuss its position in private. For example, the board team will probably want to caucus after they have heard the teachers' proposals. During this caucus, they can discuss the teachers' requests, think about their positions on the issues, and formulate a response to give to the teachers when they return to the table.

6. Contrary to the usual procedure of having only one spokesperson for a team, it is suggested that the team members alternate this responsibility in order to give everyone this experience. Or the team can let each member present a proposal or part of a proposal at the table.

7. Depending on the time available, the instructor can decide whether all proposals should be in writing or can be given orally.

8. The teams should bargain until they agree on a "contract" or until time expires. The leader may want to give the participants time to describe their experiences, their feelings about the process, whether they enjoyed or felt uncomfortable in the simulation, and what items were included in the final contracts that were completed.

9. From time to time, questions will come up about the district, budget, past experience, and other items not included in the description. It has worked well in the past to tell the participants that they may assume what they wish as long as they tell the other side.

BACKGROUND INFORMATION

The simulation involves Rockville, a small city in the Midwest. It is basically a middle-class city with some lower-income citizens, most of whom work in factories in a larger nearby city. The people of Rockville seem to support the school district, although the number of adults who have students in the schools appears to decline yearly. The income level and education level for Rockville is average for a city this size.

The city consists mostly of single-family homes, some apartments, and small businesses (hardware stores, drug stores, car dealers). There are a few companies but no heavy industry or large shopping centers. A substantial portion of the area is covered by a beautiful national forest.

The Rockville School District consists of four high schools, six middle schools, and thirty-one elementary schools and is governed by a board of education. The seven board members are elected for staggered terms and by different areas of the city.

The buildings in the district have been well maintained through the years, although an increasing amount of money has to be devoted to this cause every year.

Approximately 45 percent of the budget comes from local property taxes, 50 percent from state funds, and 5 percent from federal funds. Any increases in local property taxes must be approved by the voters of the district. Although the citizens have been supportive of increased taxes for the schools in the past, the two most recent requests for increases were defeated by a margin of 60 percent to 40 percent and a narrower margin of 55 percent to 45 percent. No increase has been placed on the ballot for this year.

The teacher's organization, the Rockville Education Association (REA), is affiliated with the national association and represents more than 70 percent of the teachers. Although there have been representative challenges from time to time, these have not been serious ones and the REA has maintained a strong position with the teachers.

The board of education and the REA are concluding the second year of a two-year contract and are ready to negotiate a new contract. Relationships between the two groups have been fairly good, although the teachers have complained about class size and have filed grievances (unsuccessfully) dealing with preparation periods at the elementary school level.

Statistics

Schools in the District

4 high schools (grades 9–12) with a total enrollment of	6,125
6 middle schools (grades 6–8) with a total enrollment of	5,506
31 elementary schools (grades K–5) with an enrollment of	14,284
Total: 41 schools with an enrollment of	25,915

Professional Personnel

High school administrators	12
High school teachers, counselors, librarians, others	312
Middle school administrators	18
Middle school teachers, counselors, librarians, others	220
Elementary school administrators	43
Elementary school teachers, counselors, librarians, others	580
Central-office staff	
Superintendent	1
Assistant superintendents	3
Other administrators	25

Budget

Property in this district is assessed at 35 percent of market (sale) value. Reassessment of property was completed last year, and the district's assessed valuation increased significantly. However, due to the state's law on the rollback of property taxes, this increase in assessed valuation did not yield much of an increase in local tax revenue. Basically, the only way to increase revenue is to have the electorate pass a tax levy increase or to receive an increase in state funds. Last year, the district received additional state funding that eased the financial condition of the district. This year, the amount from the state should be about the same since there is a slight decline in enrollment.

The district's budget is balanced; revenues and expenses are nearly equal. The carryover of funds (revenues minus expenses for the year) should be between 2 and 3 percent of the budget.

In the past couple of years, the district has reduced the number of teachers and administrators and eliminated some programs in order to maintain a balanced budget. Any significant increases in the budget will necessitate additional local taxes or additional reductions in staffing.

Salary Schedule

The salary schedule for the district is included in the master contract, which is the appendix to this chapter. Data from nearby schools are included in figure. 11.1.

Figure II.I. Data from Nearby School Districts.

	Rockville	Freetown	Brownstown	Westfield
Enrollment	25,915	29,634	34,441	32,379
Starting Salary	$30,000	$29,400	$30,600	$29,700
Maximum Salary	$54,000	$51,500	$56,000	$53,000
Extra pay for extra duties?	no	no	yes	yes
Board pays medical?	yes, ¾	yes, ¾	yes, full	yes, full
Duty-free lunch period?	no	yes	yes	no
At least two prep periods per week?	no	yes	no	yes
Class-size limit?	no	no	yes	no

Issues for Negotiations

1. Salary increases.
2. Medical. The teachers want to increase the extent of the board's payment toward medical insurance. The current insurance costs $4,500 per teacher, which is shared by the teacher (25 percent) and board (75 percent).
3. Duty-free lunch period. The teachers want all teachers to have a duty-free lunch period. Currently, some of the teachers have a duty-free lunch period and the amount of time varies with the school. Elementary teachers eat lunch with their students and supervise them. There is no state law regarding this issue.
4. Preparation periods. The teachers want all teachers to have preparation periods. Currently, almost all high school teachers have one fifty-minute prep period per day; elementary teachers have none. Sometimes junior-high teachers are assigned supervision during some of their prep time.
5. Class size. The teachers want some limit placed on class sizes. Currently, there is no policy.
6. No issues are listed for the board team. The board team should examine the master contract (in the appendix to this chapter) for items it wishes to change or items it believes should be in the contract but that have not been included in the past. The board team should formulate these items into proposals to present to the teachers.

DISCUSSION QUESTIONS

1. How did you feel about the simulation experience?
2. Do you think you would like to negotiate "for real"?
3. Did your final contract reflect what you hoped it would be?
4. Did you and your team have any difficulty in agreeing on the team's positions?
5. Did you feel comfortable being the spokesperson?
6. Did you spend a lot of time in caucuses? Were you surprised at the amount of time?
7. Did you have enough time to finish?
8. What would have made the simulation better?

APPENDIX

MASTER CONTRACT

between the

ROCKVILLE EDUCATION ASSOCIATION

and the

ROCKVILLE BOARD OF EDUCATION

20___–20___

TABLE OF CONTENTS

(Only a few of the sections of the master contract are included here. A full contract would have many other sections. The sections included here are not meant to be "ideal" examples because they are to be used in the simulation.)

I. RECOGNITION

The Board of Education of the Rockville School District, hereinafter referred to as the Board, recognizes the Rockville Education Association (REA), hereinafter referred to as the Association, as the sole and exclusive bargaining agent for the teachers in the Rockville School District.

II. SCOPE OF NEGOTIATIONS

The Association and the Board agree to bargain in good faith with respect to all items in this Contract and any which either party feels is a matter of concern, provided such obligation does not compel either party to agree to a proposal or require the making of a concession.

III. GRIEVANCE PROCEDURE

1. Definitions:

  a. A grievance is any complaint which a teacher has with the administration of the school or the district.
  b. A grievant shall mean either an individual member or group of members of the bargaining unit having the same grievance.
  c. "Days" referred to will be construed to mean actual business days on which the central office is open.

2. Procedure:

Level 1: The grievant shall file the grievance in writing with the building principal within twenty days of the day the grievance arises. The building principal shall confer with the grievant in an attempt to resolve the grievance within five days of the filing. A decision, in writing, shall be sent to the grievant within five days of this conference.

Level 2: If the grievant is not satisfied with the grievance response at Level 1, the grievant may appeal to the superintendent in writing within ten days after receipt of the Level 1 response from the principal. The superintendent or his or her designee shall hold a conference within ten days after the filing of the appeal, and a written decision shall be sent to the grievant within five days of this conference.

Level 3: If the grievant is not satisfied with the grievance response at Level 2, the grievant may appeal to the Board within ten days after receipt of the Level 2 response from the superintendent. Within ten days after the receipt of the appeal, the Board shall hold a conference with the grievant. The Board shall send a written response to the grievant within ten days of this conference.

Level 4: If the grievant is not satisfied with the grievance response at Level 3, the grievant may submit the grievance to arbitration before an arbitrator chosen by the parties hereto. The decision of the arbitrator shall be binding upon both parties. The cost of any arbitration shall be shared equally by the parties.

IV. DUTY-FREE LUNCH PERIOD

While the Board recognizes that it would be ideal for every teacher in the District to have a duty-free lunch period, it also recognizes that it has an obligation to properly supervise its students in the lunchrooms, playgrounds, and classrooms in the District. Therefore, it shall be the practice for principals to make an effort to schedule a duty-free lunch period for teachers at the middle school and high school whenever possible. At the elementary schools, it is expected that teachers will be assigned supervisory responsibilities during some of their lunch periods.

V. PREPARATION PERIODS

While the Board recognizes the usefulness of a preparation period for teachers, it also notes the difficulty of providing such, especially at the elementary school level. High school teachers, when possible, will be given a fifty-minute preparation period daily; middle school teachers will be given a preparation period daily, although some such periods may be reassigned for supervisory purposes when the principal deems it necessary. Since elementary teachers do not have time schedules similar to those of middle and high school teachers but do have music and art pull-outs from time to time, no regular preparation period will be assigned elementary teachers.

VI. TEACHER EVALUATION

Procedures:

1. Evaluation of the teacher shall be conducted for the purpose of improving instruction. Criticism should be constructive and accompanied by suggestions for improvement.
2. The building principal will formally, in writing, evaluate each nontenured teacher annually. The building principal will formally, in writing, evaluate each tenured teacher at the principal's discretion, but at least once every three years.
3. A copy of the evaluation shall be given to the teacher, and a conference shall be held between the teacher and the building principal within ten days following the second formal observation. A copy signed by both parties shall be retained by the teacher and the administration.
4. If the teacher feels his or her evaluation is incomplete, inaccurate, or unjust, he or she may put these objections in writing and have them attached to the evaluation report to be placed in the personnel file within thirty days. A copy signed by both parties shall be retained by the teacher.
5. Each formal written evaluation shall be preceded by at least two classroom observations of at least twenty minutes each.
6. Included in each teacher's evaluation shall be a section for informal observation of the teacher's extracurricular assignments.
7. Observation of all teacher duties, assignments, and responsibilities shall be conducted with the knowledge of the teacher.

VII. SALARY

The salary schedule, as agreed upon by both parties, is attached as Appendix A.

VIII. MEDICAL BENEFITS

The Board will agree to maintain the current medical coverage for all full-time teachers and will pay seventy-five percent of the total premium for such coverage. Should the premium increase during the term of this contract, the Board will agree to pay seventy-five percent of that increase.

IX. JOB SHARING

The phrase "job sharing" shall mean two bargaining unit members sharing one job. For any job sharer working over fifty percent, the Board shall pay health insurance for that teacher equal to half the percentage paid to other full-time teachers.

X. DURATION

This Contract shall be effective on (date), 20___ and shall continue in full force and effect until (date), 20___. On or before (date), 20___, either party may notify the other of its intent to modify, change, or amend this Contract. This Contract shall remain in full force and effect throughout these negotiations.

APPENDIX A   Salary Schedule

Step	BA	BA+15	MA	MA+15	MA+30	MA+45
0	$30,000	$31,000	$32,500	$33,500	$34,500	$36,000
1	30,500	31,500	33,500	34,500	35,700	37,500
2	31,000	32,000	34,500	35,500	36,900	39,000
3	31,500	32,500	35,500	36,500	38,100	40,500
4	32,000	33,000	36,500	37,500	39,300	42,000
5	32,500	33,500	37,500	38,500	40,500	43,500
6	33,000	34,000	38,500	39,500	41,700	45,000
7	33,500	34,500	39,500	40,500	42,900	46,500
8		35,000	40,500	41,500	44,100	48,000
9		35,500	41,500	42,500	45,300	49,500
10			42,500	43,500	46,500	51,000
11			43,500	44,500	47,700	52,500
12				45,500	48,900	54,000

APPENDIX:
THE FATE OF PUBLIC EDUCATION

Clete R. Bulach and William L. Sharp

The following essay presents one view of teacher unions and the role they could have in the future. A condensed version of this essay was published on the opinion/editorial page of the New York Times *on May 11, 1989. Some of the predictions made in this essay have come true today. A "comments" section has been added for this edition of the book.*

The fate of public education as we know it now, for better or worse, lies partially in the hands of the teacher unions. Teacher unions in many states have become increasingly more militant, and this militancy poses a number of problems for boards of education. These problems include contractual constraints on the board, lower priority of service to clients, and a perceived decline in quality.

Negotiated contracts between teachers and the board have placed constraints upon the board, limiting the ability of administrators and boards to improve the quality of instruction. For example, in many states, if the board wants to lengthen the school day for students or change the bell schedule, these changes must be negotiated. When the board and administrators attempt to respond to the increasing criticism of public education, they find that their hands are tied by contractual constraints.

One of the most damaging results of teacher militancy is the shift in emphasis from service to clients (students) to taking care of the needs of the teachers. Verbally, many union leaders will tell you that schools exist for students, but in practice, especially at the bargaining table, schools exist to provide jobs. For example, when some boards have proposed increasing the requirements in areas such as English or mathematics, union leaders have opposed these changes because some teachers may lose their jobs even though other teachers will be hired. Their number one concern is job security.

This shift away from service to clients is in direct proportion to the degree of teacher militancy, and is concomitant with a growing decline in teacher professionalism. A professional has a strong desire, a compulsion, to serve the client whose needs take precedence over the needs of the person providing the service. If teacher unions continue to be more concerned with the needs of their members and with the union organization itself than they are about the needs of the students, a decline in the quality of public education will result.

As parents detect or think they detect this decline in quality, more and more insist on alternatives to the education currently available. A recent study by Esposito shows that twenty-three states have adopted or may adopt some type of plan involving "educational choice," defined as parental selection among public schools. A number of states are considering the Minnesota plan, which allows parents to choose the school their child will attend. Such a plan would end public education as we know it today. Some schools would lose students and teachers and encounter a funding crisis; others would have more students than they could handle, causing them to rid themselves of poor academic students and create, as a result, elitist schools. The American comprehensive community high school would die.

The leaders of the two national teacher unions have written on reform and the role of the union. Mary Futrell, president of the NEA, suggests three strategies and twelve guidelines for improving schools, emphasizing the role of the members of NEA, but not mentioning the effect of these strategies and guidelines upon students. Again, Futrell seems more concerned about her membership than students.

Albert Shanker, president of the rival AFT, takes a different approach. In a recent *New York Times* column, he discussed a RAND report and stated that strong union leadership is essential in order to make the necessary changes in classroom reforms which affect students. While Shanker certainly does not advocate weaker unions, he does suggest that teachers, with proper union leadership, can constructively influence reform. In fact, his column on the study states that ". . . it was in the strong-union districts that the union played the most constructive and far-reaching role in reform."

Teacher unions do not have to become weaker; they have to change their priorities: toward greater professionalism, toward a greater concern for the welfare and learning of students, toward a balance of power with less concern for their organizational needs. If unions begin to use their power to cooperate in the reform effort instead of fighting it, they will get support from sources they have forgotten lately: parents, administrators, the business community, and boards of education. And, as these groups work cooperatively to reform the schools and help the students, both the schools and the unions will become stronger and win back community respect and support.

COMMENTS

As stated in the introduction to this essay, some of the predictions made in 1989 have come true. The two major teacher unions have continued to emphasize membership over concern for students, to the extent that alternatives to traditional public education have become very popular. Home schooling has increased greatly, and parents and politicians alike have pushed for charter schools, tuition tax credits, vouchers, privatization of schools, and performance contracting. Myron Lieberman, in his recent book, states that the NEA and AFT do not want anything to reduce their influence, membership, or revenues and thus oppose the alternatives just mentioned.[1] Lieberman contends that the NEA has become very political, possessing great influence at the state and national governmental levels and reflecting the "agenda of the most liberal wing of the Democratic Party."[2] He mentions that the NEA has thirty-three different caucuses—organizations within the NEA that have been established to promote their causes. The interesting one that he mentions is the Republican Caucus. While one might expect that this caucus, like others, would seek to promote its cause (the Republican Party) within the NEA, on the contrary, it is used to maximize the influence of the NEA within the Republican Party. And, in 1994, this Republican Caucus endorsed only Democratic Party candidates for NEA offices. In 1996, the NEA political action committee endorsed 250 Democratic candidates for Congress and one Republican.[3]

Many citizens today look at the national teacher unions and see them as roadblocks to educational reform, and as organizations dedicated to their own survival and power. The state of Indiana has tried to pass various pieces of educational reform, some successfully, but the state organization for the NEA, the Indiana State Teachers Association (ISTA), has fought against many of these reforms. The *Indianapolis Star,* in a special section on education in 2002, discussed some of the reform efforts from years past and stated the following: "Chief among those standing in the way, and proud of it, was Bob Margraf, then the top lobbyist for ISTA. 'By the time [Governor] Bob Orr had A-Plus [a reform package], there was no question about who was the most powerful lobbying group in the state,' Margraf boasted. 'The floor of the House was controlled by ISTA.'"[4] The ISTA targeted those legislators who opposed them (and who supported educational reform) and spent $463,000 to defeat them in the next election. Quoting Margraf again, "You get one shot at [the] ISTA. . . . We said these are people we're going to beat, and we beat them. They won the issue. They lost the leadership [of the legislature]. Who's the biggest loser?" The *Star* concludes by saying that the biggest loser may be the public, meaning the children.[5]

NOTES

1. Myron Lieberman, *The Teacher Unions: How They Sabotage Educational Reform and Why* (San Francisco: Encounter, 2000).

2. Lieberman, *Teacher Unions,* 35.

3. Lieberman, *Teacher Unions,* 39.

4. Mary Beth Schneider, "The Long Conflict over Reform," in a special report on education, "A Promise Broken: Failing Indiana's Schoolchildren," *Indianapolis Star,* September 15, 2002, S5.

5. Schneider, "Long Conflict," S5.

GLOSSARY

Agency shop A condition of employment under which all bargaining-unit employees are required to pay a fair-share fee if they do not join the union.

Arbitration, Advisory A decision made by a neutral third party that may or may not be accepted.

Arbitration, Binding A decision made by a neutral third party that must be accepted by both sides.

Bargaining unit A group composed of a number of employees who bargain together. A school may have a number of bargaining units.

Boilerplate A proposal submitted at negotiation sessions throughout the state; often given by a state association to all the local unions.

Caucus A private meeting (during negotiations) during which one side meets to formulate strategy and responses.

Cease and desist order A decision by the state employment relations board telling the guilty party to stop similar actions in the future.

Chief negotiator The person who speaks for the negotiations team at the table.

Collective bargaining A formal situation in which management and union discuss salary and working conditions in order to arrive at a written contract.

Contract A written document that covers all the issues agreed upon by management and labor; also called a master contract, agreement, and other names.

Crossing teachers Those teachers who have decided to "cross the picket line" and work during a strike.

Exclusive representative (or exclusive bargaining agent) The group that has been elected by the union membership to represent them in bargaining.

Fact-finding The process in which a neutral third party gathers information from management and labor and makes recommendations for solutions.

Fair share An amount of money, similar to union dues, required of those under agency shop.

Good faith bargaining Negotiations in which the parties meet at reasonable times and places and honestly attempt to resolve issues.

Grievance An alleged violation of the contract.

Impasse The condition in which no progress is being made in collective bargaining.

"Lieutenant Columbo" routine The situation in which one side tries to add an issue late in negotiations.

Lockout Action taken by management to close the institution (school) to employees.

Management rights clause A section of the contract that details the rights of the board of education. Examples are given in chapter 5.

Mandatory *See* Scope of bargaining.

Mediation The process in which a neutral third party attempts to get management and labor to agree on issues.

Meet and confer A type of meeting in which management and employees discuss salary and working conditions informally. The results of the meeting are not binding and may not be in written form.

Memorandum of Understanding A letter that is not part of the contract (side letter) but expresses the agreed-upon position of both sides on some issue. An example is given in chapter 6.

Negotiations *See* Collective bargaining.

Packages, Negotiating A method of negotiations in which several issues from each side are grouped together as one proposal. An example is given in chapter 5.

Permissive *See* Scope of bargaining.

Private sector Pertains to employees, such as industrial and business workers, who are paid from nontax funds.

Probable cause A determination that either management or labor may have committed an unfair labor practice.

Prohibited *See* Scope of bargaining.

Public sector Pertains to employees who are paid from tax funds, such as school teachers.

Reopener A clause in the contract that states an area that can be renegotiated under specified conditions.

Representative election The selection of the group that will represent the employees.

Scope of bargaining The extent to which the parties must bargain: some issues are mandatory and must be negotiated; some issues are permissive and may be negotiated; and some issues are prohibited and cannot be negotiated.

Sidebar A private talk, away from the negotiations table, usually between the chief negotiators of both sides.

Side letter *See* Memorandum of Understanding.

State employment relations board Based on the National Labor Relations Board concept, these state boards make rules for public-sector bargaining and unfair labor practices.

Unfair labor practice Action by either the employer or the employee organization that is in violation of the rights established by the state employment relations board.

Unilateral action by board Action taken by the board of education without negotiations with the union.

Union shop A condition under which all members of the bargaining unit must join and retain membership in the union to remain employed.

Win–win bargaining A nonconfrontational alternative to the usual collective bargaining process. Chapter 8 describes this process.

Zipper clause A section of the contract that states that everything that has been agreed upon is contained in the contract. An example is given in chapter 6.

SUGGESTED READINGS

Andree, Robert G. *Collective Negotiations*. Lexington, Mass.: Heath, 1970.
———. *The Art of Negotiation*. Lexington, Mass.: Heath, 1971.
Ashby, Lloyd W., James E. McGinnis, and Thomas E. Persing. *Common Sense in Negotiations*. Danville, Ill.: Interstate, 1972.
Bent, Alan E., and T. Zane Reeves. *Collective Bargaining in the Public Sector*. Menlo Park, Calif.: Benjamin Cummings, 1978.
Bornstein, Tim. *Facts about Fact Finding*. Washington, D.C.: Labor-Management Relations Service, 1973.
Cresswell, Anthony M., and Michael J. Murphy. *Education and Collective Bargaining*. Berkeley, Calif.: McCuthan, 1976.
Elam, Stanley M., Myron Lieberman, and Michael H. Moskow. *Collective Negotiations in Public Education*. Chicago: Rand McNally, 1967.
Kearney, R. C. *Labor Relations in the Public Sector*. New York: Dekker, 2001.
Lieberman, Myron. *Before, during, and after Bargaining*. Chicago: Teach 'em, 1979.
———. *The Teacher Unions: How They Sabotage Educational Reform and Why*. San Francisco: Encounter, 2000.
Miller, William C., and David N. Newbury. *Teacher Negotiations: A Guide for Bargaining Teams*. West Nyack, NY: Parker, 1970.
———. Ohio Public Employees Collective Bargaining Law and Rules. Columbus: Ohio State Employment Relations Board, 1988.
O'Reilly, Robert C.. *Readings in Public School Collective Bargaining*. Washington, D.C.: Educational Service Bureau, 1971.

———. *Understanding Collective Bargaining in Education.* Metuchen, N.J.: Scarecrow, 1978.

Schneider, Mary Beth. "The Long Conflict over Reform." In a special report on education, "A Promise Broken: Failing Indiana's Schoolchildren," September 15, 2002.

Sharkey, Samuel M., Jr. *Public Employee Strikes: Causes and Effects.* Washington D.C.: Labor-Management Relations Service, 1970.

Sharp, William L. "The Role of the Superintendent and School Board in Collective Bargaining: 1989–1999." Paper presented at the annual meeting of the Mid-Western Educational Research Association, Chicago, October 14, 1999.

State Employee Relations Board. SERB Annual Report 2001, Columbus: Ohio State Employment Relations Board, 2001.

Stinnett, T. M., Jack H. Kleinmann, and Martha L. Ware. *Professional Negotiation in Public Education.* New York: Macmillan, 1966.

Warner, Kenneth O., ed. *Collective Bargaining in the Public Service: Theory and Practice.* Chicago: Public Personnel Association, 1967.

Zack, Arnold M. *Public Sector Mediation.* Washington, D.C.: Bureau of National Affairs, 1985.

INDEX

ABOUT THE CONTRIBUTORS

Clete R. Bulach is an associate professor of educational leadership at the State University of West Georgia at Carrollton, and is chief executive officer of the Professional Development and Assessment Center consulting agency. Prior to that, he was at Murray State University in Murray, Kentucky, and served as a superintendent for fourteen years in Ohio. He also taught collective bargaining as an adjunct professor at the University of Akron in Akron, Ohio. As a superintendent, he served as the chief negotiator for three different boards of education. As a teacher in Cincinnati public schools (1964–1970), he served as an officer in the Cincinnati Federation of Teachers and was on the teachers' negotiating team. Bulach's article was original for this book.

Karen M. Moriarty was the assistant superintendent for personnel of Consolidated High School District 230, a three-high-school district in southwest Cook County, Illinois, when the win–win bargaining negotiations she describes took place. The district population consists of nearly 6,000 students and 660 employees, for which there are five recognized unions/associations for the bargaining units of teachers, secretarial personnel, maintenance workers, bus drivers, and food-service employees. The district had experienced a five-day teachers' strike in each of the previous two contract years, 1980 and 1982, prior to the win–win experience in 1984. Moriarty's article, previously unpublished, was presented as a paper at the Annual Meeting of the Association of Negotiators and Contract Administrators in Clearwater Beach, Florida, November 7–9, 1984.

Vicki Braden Sharp, Ph.D., has been an educator with Indianapolis Public Schools since 1970 and is a licensed teacher, counselor, clinical social worker, marriage and family therapist, psychologist, and administrator. For the past ten years, she has been successful in negotiating contracts involving the federal government for Watters and Associates.

ABOUT THE AUTHOR

William Sharp is professor of educational leadership at Ball State University, Muncie, Indiana, and was previously a professor in the Department of Educational Administration and Higher Education and associate dean of the College of Education at Southern Illinois University at Carbondale. Prior to this position, he was an associate professor at the University of Akron and was a school superintendent in Indiana and Illinois before his university positions. During his superintendencies, *Executive Educator* selected him as one of the top 100 superintendents in the country. He has an B.A. in mathematics and an M.S. in secondary education from Indiana University, a graduate diploma from Durham University in England, where he was a Durham Scholar, and a Ph.D. from Northwestern University. He has had articles published in numerous education journals, *The New York Times*, and the *Cleveland Plain Dealer.* He has written two books, *Collective Bargaining in the Public Schools* and *Winning at Collective Bargaining: Strategies Everyone Can Live With,* and he has co-authored the following books with James K. Walter: *The Principal As School Manager; The School Superintendent: The Profession and the Person; Case Studies for School Leaders: Implementing the ISLLC Standards*; and *The Principal As School Manager, Second Edition.*